PROVERSITY™

PROVERSITY™

Getting Past Face Value and
Finding the Soul of People
—A Manager's Journey

Lawrence Otis Graham

JOHN WILEY & SONS, INC.
New York • Chichester • Weinheim • Brisbane • Singapore • Toronto

To Pamela—the best friend and the best role model that a husband could ever have.

CONTENTS

Contents

INTRODUCTION

Four years ago, I was working as a corporate attorney in one of the largest law firms in New York City while simultaneously completing research on a book that surveyed the employment practices of the most respected corporations in the Fortune 1000. It was during that time that I received the biggest lesson of my life on the hidden barriers that exist for so many people in corporate America.

One of these barriers is called *Passive Bias,* a term that I coined. I discovered this phenomenon when, as a part of my book research, I took a leave of absence from my law firm job, disguised my resume, and began working undercover as a busboy at an all-white Connecticut country club that discriminated against blacks, women, Jews, Asians, Hispanics, and others.

My experience in this Connecticut club was a disturbing one—not because it revealed how the club world keeps minorities, women, and others off the golf course and outside an environment of powerful networks. It was disturbing because there I saw some of the most prominent executives in corporate America spend Saturday and Sunday at an institution that they knew actively discriminated on the grounds of race, gender, ethnicity, and religion, yet they arrived at work Monday morning operating under the notion that they could fairly hire, manage, and evaluate their employees on a color-blind, gender-blind, religion-blind basis.

The fact that this practice went on—and continues to go on—in many parts of the country, unchallenged, told me that either there are great numbers of "schizophrenic" managers who honestly believe they can be weekend bigots, and then transform themselves into open-minded team builders in the workplace, or that many managers and employees working in our organizations are simply unaware of the bias that they, themselves, adopt and practice.

Recognizing that the decision to erase deeply held, biased attitudes about others lies with the individual, I wrote this book to offer a new approach to addressing "diversity" in organizations and the customers they serve.

Whether you are a part of a large corporation, a governmental agency, a nonprofit group, an educational institution, or a small business, you certainly have recognized how much the marketplace around you has changed. But you may have been blindsided, victimized, or confused by the debate over embracing diversity and celebrating differences.

After four years of research on managing diverse organizations and working with managers at all tenure levels through my consulting firm, Progressive Management Associates, Inc., I have discovered that organizations have been misplacing their resources as they adapt to new human resources challenges. Rather than focusing on the diversity—or differences—among workers, they should instead adapt a more unifying approach and focus on *Proversity,* the characteristics that people in their organizations have *in common. Proversity* is quite simply Progressive Diversity:

Proversity™ \ *noun* **1.** progressive diversity: the product of bringing together individuals who appear different, but who have many common characteristics. **2.** a more advanced and progressive form of diversity planning. **3.** a description of individuals who look different on the exterior, but are actually quite similar. **4.** the condition of having similar characteristics on a deep level in spite of existing surface characteristics that look different.

I wrote this book for managers and organizations who are trying to remain both competitive and responsible in the face of four major challenges:

1. A pressure to serve increasingly diverse customers.
2. A need to hire and train diverse workers.
3. A desire to address the ongoing reversal of affirmative action policies.
4. The urge to build a cohesive organization in spite of these changes.

Organizations are more likely to succeed at addressing these four challenges once they are able to teach their workers to conduct themselves as Progressive Managers.

I use the term *Progressive Manager*™ to describe any employee or worker who adopts Proversity strategies and recognizes that the best managers are those who look beyond what is different about themselves, their coworkers and consumers, and who attempt to find the goals and interests that they all have in common. The Progressive Manager understands that an organization's success can be threatened by those employees who practice any type of *passive bias*— bigotry that seems benign and that is not intended to harm or insult others.

I have coined the terms *passive bias* and *Proversity* to help the Progressive Manager find his or her own strengths while also inspiring coworkers to find theirs.

I wrote this book in the format of a story—a story of a young manager who is probably not very different from people we have met in our own organizations.

As you get to know Percy McGee, this average manager in an average American company, and follow him through his experiences and interactions with coworkers and others, you will see how Progressive Managers get their workers to overcome passive bias in the workplace and use the power of Proversity to become more productive and more successful in this increasingly changing world. I believe we can all benefit from the lessons that Percy McGee learns in these pages.

Part One

AN ORGANIZATION WITH PASSIVE BIAS

1

Those Were
the Days

"What happened to the way things used to be?"

This was the question that was always on the mind of Percy McGee. As he sat in his corner office looking out into the hallway beyond his secretary's desk, he thought about how much his company, his department—even his floor—had changed since he arrived fourteen years ago.

Moving his way up through the entry-level and middle-level management ranks of the 99-year-old National Flashlight Company (NFC) was a challenge that Percy had enjoyed meeting. As Vice President of Domestic Marketing, he was becoming a respected and valued executive, and was finally catching the eye of the CEO. He felt it was just a matter of time before he would be tapped for a senior executive spot at NFC; he was sure they were grooming him for that.

As Percy considered his status in the organization—a business with operations in nine countries—he stared up at the company logo statuette sitting on his desk: a one-and-a-half-foot high bald eagle with outstretched wings—one of the most patriotic symbols of America. Some said that there was something anachronistic about the NFC company statue—a brass bald eagle perched next to a primitive torch with the company's motto hanging across the statue's base: National Flashlight Company: Lighting Our Nation From Sea to Shining Sea.

While Percy felt that the American Bald Eagle and the company motto paid appropriate respect to NFC's American roots, some thought it missed the point, particularly since the $2.4 billion business had long been a multinational corporation. The nationalistic symbols clearly needed some reworking. In fact, during recent years, several of the new marketing executives and even outside vendors suggested that the large and awkward statue be redesigned to include a new motto and symbol that better reflected NFC's international presence. In spite of the criticisms, the statue seemed just fine to Percy, and it maintained a prominent place on his desk.

Although he was a young manager, he was like some of NFC's older executives who found comfort in holding onto NFC's past. For them, it was the all-American company with the all-American heritage. Like them, Percy saw value in nostalgia, and the NFC eagle statue was a part of that nostalgia. "Even if it does seem flawed today," Percy often said, "we shouldn't be going around altering things that our company's founders created. Let's act with moderation and try to leave things as they are."

In fact, that was Percy's response to many of the suggestions that were being offered by the newer vendors and managers who worked with or joined the company. He often recoiled at their suggestions on how NFC should pursue its marketing or other strategies. To him, their progressive strategies seemed radical and unrealistic. And to thwart these potential changes, he responded to new workers and new ideas with that same answer, "Let's act with moderation and try to leave things as they are."

NFC had been a good company for Percy, and he saw no reason to change the organization or the way it was run. In fact, he believed that it was NFC's resistance to industry fads and fickle consumer behavior that had made it possible for the company to outlast its competitors for so many years. And no one was a better chronicler of NFC's history than Percy.

In fact, Percy's ties to the company dated back to when he was a 12-year-old Boy Scout. His scoutmaster had given each new troop member an NFC "Eagle Eye" flashlight, and even today, twenty-eight years later, that metal flashlight sat on Percy's desk.

Percy was devastated when the company discontinued the "Eagle Eye" model design three years ago. "That light has been around forever," he complained, "and I see no reason to change the design."

NFC had been a good company and he saw no reason to change it.

And that was Percy's attitude today about NFC: The way that things used to be was the way things ought to be. And why would anyone be surprised that he felt this way? Anyone could see that Percy had lived a pleasant and stable life with little turmoil, and virtually no changes or surprises. He had been the all-American kid, who had developed all-American aspirations. He had worked his way into a top manager's job at the all-American company.

But even with all his personal success, the young manager was beginning to sense that something was going wrong with the company around him. He was perfectly content with his own department's success, but what made him uneasy was what went on outside his office. Things didn't seem normal anymore and they made him feel more uneasy each year—particularly as he began to see how his employer was expanding and changing.

As he looked up from the eagle statuette and out into the hallway shaking his head, he ran his hand across the spiral-bound sales reports on his desk and whispered to himself, "What happened to the way things used to be?"

During the past two years, Percy had asked himself that question so many times, he could sometimes think of nothing else. Whether sitting through department meetings, walking through the company cafeteria or even just riding the elevator up to his office, he found himself asking the same question, "What happened to the way things used to be?" As he saw new people coming into the company, new policies implemented by personnel, new people appearing in company advertisements, and even new rules for the support staff's dress code, he wondered why things had to keep changing.

He thought about the old NFC and all the things that he had liked about it:

- He thought of Sammy, the elderly black man who was contracted by NFC to walk the halls every Monday and Thursday, offering shoe shines to the employees who sat at their desks. Even when sitting in his leather desk chair talking on the phone or running a meeting,

Percy could count on the good-natured Sammy to work diligently and quietly on his knees without disturbing the conversation or interrupting Percy's train of thought. But shoe shine visits were eliminated after several of the new black employees complained that Sammy's role created a demeaning and racist atmosphere.

- He thought of the old executive dining room that was reserved for any manager with a title of Director or above. Percy liked the idea of not having to eat alongside clerical staff, entry-level workers, and others who had been relegated to the larger and noisier company cafeteria. But the executive dining room had been closed four years ago after a "quality of life" committee had performed a cultural audit and declared that separate lunchrooms gave rise to elitist attitudes in the office.

- He thought of the color-coordinated uniform smocks that certain members of the support staff used to wear at the office. Mailroom people had blue smocks, photocopy staff wore green, internal messengers wore red, cleaning staff wore white, security workers wore brown, and fax room staff wore black. Percy had liked the system because it relieved him from having to remember faces or names. The CEO eliminated the uniforms after a group of support staff workers complained that the smocks depersonalized them and made them feel unappreciated.

- He thought of Luigi, the 80-year-old Italian man that used to act as the company barber. For thirty-five years, he visited the executives every Wednesday and Friday, offering to cut hair in their private offices before work or during the lunch hour. That service was eliminated six years ago as NFC's pool of female executives grew and insisted that it was sexist for the company to offer a barber to the men and not offer a salon for the women.

- He thought of the Annual NFC Christmas and Mistletoe Party that used to be preceded by a week of "Secret Santa" gift giving between employees and the decorating of the company's 35-foot Christmas tree in the building's main lobby. Four years ago, several workers commented that they were not Christians and that it seemed insensitive for the company to celebrate Christmas and not the holidays of their respective religions. They soon renamed the event a Holiday Party, and they eliminated the Christmas tree and the "Secret Santa" gift giving, and replaced it with a food drive for a local homeless shelter.

- He also thought of the way he and his fellow colleagues used to tell jokes in the hallway or in weekly planning meetings without having to worry that some woman or some minority person might get offended. Since they had all been white men, they could tell an occasional off-color sexual, ethnic, or racial joke without looking over their shoulder or without wondering who else was in the room. But ever since large numbers of women and minorities began walking those halls and participating in those meetings, an ad hoc NFC sensitivity taskforce had concluded that jokes of a racial or sexual nature should be forbidden as they created a hostile work environment for fellow minority and female employees.

Yes, those days were gone.

A number of his old friends had left NFC for the White Light Manufacturing Company, a light bulb company that had been started nine years ago by several former NFC managers who felt that NFC had begun to change its "conservative direction." The executives at White Light had resisted the changes that the new CEO had been implementing and they had agreed that their new company was going to be cautious about the people they hired and the policies they established in the running of the new company. Operating in a suburban office complex in a remote area, White Light had no desire to hire or serve people outside the United States, and it had no desire to establish the diverse workforce that was now growing at NFC.

Percy was becoming well aware of the changing NFC workforce. He saw all these different people—black, Hispanic, Asian, Native American, female, foreign-born, Jewish, Muslim, over-55, disabled, homosexual—come into the company with all their "sensitivities" and "complaints"—as he called them—and he saw all the "regular" people disappear. He could almost sympathize with the executives who had left to join White Light. He could hardly think of a dozen straight, white American guys that had been hired by NFC during the latest recruiting season.

After being told repeatedly that he had to be sensitive to the fact that NFC's staff was now more varied in its racial, ethnic, gender, and religious makeup, Percy found himself getting rattled. He had nothing against all these new and different people, but he also had no prior experience in managing them or even living around them.

With NFC employing over 1,600 employees and producing over $2.4 billion in annual revenues in almost a dozen countries, the company was becoming a global organization with varied needs and very different employees. By diversifying into incandescent and fluorescent light bulbs, as well as home and office lighting fixtures, the company was finding success in more than just its original product of flashlights. In fact, flashlights now represented only 8 percent of the company's annual revenues.

Of course, Percy studied and understood the markets that NFC was reaching. He managed a department of 218 people—including the outside salespeople—and oversaw an annual budget of $42 million. Although the company's operations outside the United States were growing, Percy had long been considered one of the smartest and most ambitious young managers at the company's American headquarters. He was a success all around. An honors graduate from a Big Ten college and an Ivy League business school, at 40 he was happily married to Daisy, his high school sweetheart, the father of two young children, and an active member of his church and a volunteer scoutmaster at a local Boy Scout troop. Percy was a fast-moving star in his professional life who had virtually no barriers in his path of becoming a successful manager and executive. He was the all-American success story.

Except that Percy McGee is a Passive Bigot.

2

"Regular People" vs. "Different People"

"You know what I like about you, Ann?"

The 28-year-old executive assistant turned away from her computer monitor. "No, Mr. McGee. What's that?"

"Guess."

Ann thought for a moment. "The fact that I always get in early and stay late?"

Percy shook his head. "No, try again."

"That I never take sick days?"

"No."

"That I'm good at screening your calls and keeping bothersome vendors away from you?"

Percy shook his head again.

"Because I've got initiative and you know I can be trusted and don't have to be micromanaged every day?"

"No, Ann. You've totally missed it."

Ann frowned in confusion. "Then I don't get it. What is it that you like about me?"

"It should be pretty darned obvious, Ann. Just look at you. And look at *me*. You remind me of how this place used to be. You and me; we're like the old NFC. We're regular people."

The assistant nodded in sudden understanding. "Oh, right. No, we're not pompous at all, Mr. McGee. We're nice down-to-earth, tell-it-like-it-is people."

Percy brought his fists to his hips in mock anger and shook his head. "That's not what I mean, either. I'm not talking about who's pompous or who's down to earth. I'm not talking about *how* we are. I'm talking about *what* we are. I mean look around you."

Ann sat silently.

"We're like the old NFC. You remind me of the way things used to be at NFC. When everybody was a regular person just like you and me." Percy nodded wistfully. "Boy, when I first joined this company, things were so much simpler. You knew exactly who you were dealing with. People were just regular guys."

"Really?" Ann asked.

"Yeah, and you knew exactly who was what. That's why it took so long to find somebody like you for a secretary." Percy paused with a far-off look in his eyes. "Back when I first got here, we didn't have to comb through male secretarial applicants, or waste time interviewing folks with all these accents and worry about people taking off all these bizarre holidays. Now, nothing's normal anymore. Half the time, you get a resume, look at the name, and you don't know where these people are from—or even *what* they are. They make me interview all these people when I can just look at their names and know instantly that I'm never going to hire them."

". . . when I joined this company, things were so much simpler . . . You knew exactly who you were dealing with."

"Mr. McGee, you don't really mean that. I know you don't."

He thought back to the candidates he had interviewed five years ago. "Ann, I can remember as clear as day that each of those secretary applicants had already been screened by NFC's Secretarial Services Department. First there was Jennifer."

"And what was she like?" Ann asked.

"Well, this is how I remember the whole thing, Ann." Percy thought back to that month several years ago.

"Jennifer, it seems that you've worked for two very impressive companies before coming here to NFC. And your computer skills are great."

"Thank you, Mr. McGee," the secretarial applicant replied. "I'm familiar with all the latest office, spreadsheet, and word processing computer software and I also do shorthand and Dictaphone."

Percy nodded to himself while the young woman laid out her letters of reference.

"I've brought four letters of recommendation for you to review as well."

Percy waved away the letters with a polite gesture and thought to himself as she spoke about her last job, *Jennifer sure has a lot of hair. I wonder what she is.*

"So, where are you from Jennifer?"

The woman was surprised to be asked such a question in the midst of discussing her prior employment record, but she answered, "Oh, Elmont, just a few miles away. My parents and my siblings were all born there."

Percy had never known anyone personally from Elmont, but he heard there was a growing Jewish community there. *So, she must be Jewish. That explains the hair. I've got nothing against Jewish people, but she's probably really religious and will probably want to leave every day before sundown. And then there's all the holidays they celebrate. This won't work.*

Then there was Lydia.

"So I see you used to work for Republic Lighting, one of our old competitors," Percy remarked. "Although they are no longer in business, I like the fact that you're familiar with this industry."

"Yes," answered the applicant as she took out her resume. "Ironically, I also worked for Republic's head of marketing, so I believe I am very familiar with what your office does."

Percy was intrigued by Lydia's background of working in the light bulb business, but he noticed a slight accent in some of her words. She had wonderful diction, but her inflection was slightly different for certain words. Then it occurred to him: Lydia must be Hispanic—even though her last name was Reynolds. *I've got nothing against Hispanics, but she'll probably be on the phone all day speaking in Spanish to her friends and relatives. Then the next thing we'll find out is that she's not even legally in this country. This will never work.*

Next, Secretarial Services sent Alex.

"I'm sure you get this all the time," Percy began, "but this is the fastest typing speed I've ever seen—90 words per minute?"

"Yeah, I know it's pretty fast," said the young man as he nodded his head. "I play a pretty good piano, too."

Percy was impressed with Alex's resume and his references, but he just didn't feel comfortable offering the job to him.

"As you can see from my reference letters, I've gotten the fastest promotions of any secretary at my two prior employers." Alex handed the letters to Percy.

I don't care how fast this guy types or who recommended him, there's just no way that I can hire a man for a secretary. What kind of a guy would work as a secretary? And not that I have anything against gays, but Alex must *be gay. And the last thing I want is my secretary making passes at* me.

Percy looked up from his desk at Ann as he finished his story.

Ann offered a half-hearted smile. "Well, maybe you *were* a bit picky about who you wanted to hire, but I'm sure you didn't mean to be a bigot or anything."

"Perhaps not," Percy said, "but over the next few weeks, I turned down several other secretary candidates: Lola, because she had a slight limp, and disabled people make me feel awkward and uncomfortable. Beatrice, because although her records said she was 48, she looked like 58—and I just didn't want an unappealing looking secretary sitting outside my door. And Laura, because I just wasn't sure a black woman would fit in at a mostly white company, even though she said she'd gone to mostly white schools. But then I found you. And I knew it immediately: You looked exactly like the kind of secretary I should have."

Ann backed up toward the door and swallowed uncomfortably. "Well, Mr. McGee, of course I'm flattered that you hired me, but I think you were kind of hard on those other applicants."

Just as Percy was about to reveal one more fact to her, Ann walked back outside to her desk, closing his office door behind her.

Left alone again in his office, Percy pulled out a pad of paper and glanced up at the NFC statue. It wasn't his fault, but he couldn't help thinking about all the new people he'd had to wade through. For a split second, he had thought of telling Ann about NTO, a game he'd learned from one of his coworkers. But then he looked down at his pad of paper and realized she might not have understood.

In Percy's mind, the National Flashlight Company was changing into a total hodgepodge of odd people, and the game of NTO—Now There's One—was one of his few respites as the company continued to open its doors to more and more diverse people. Percy had learned the game from Austin Butler, an NFC salesman and one of Percy's closest friends. Austin had called the game NTO—Now There's One—because the object of the game was to stare at a group of workers or a list of employees and pick out who was "regular" and who was "different."

Percy sometimes felt bad that he was always joining in with Austin and noting how many regular people and how many other different people were around them at NFC, but he couldn't help himself. The changing makeup of NFC had become an obsession with him, and there was nothing he could do about it. So he resorted to this little ritual of NTO. Normally, he just went along quietly as the gregarious, and sometimes awkward, Austin played it in Percy's office while thumbing through the company directory or face book, but lately Percy had used his own solitary moments to note the RKO—Regular Kind Of—People and the DKO—Different Kind Of—People in the company.

NTO was a diversion that Austin and Percy used during a lull in a meeting or phone conversation. It was a solitary activity they could play on a pad of paper after having an argument with a vendor or customer. It was catalyst, sedative, ice breaker, and comic relief all wrapped into one.

Each round of NTO was a time-filler that required nothing more than a pencil, a sheet of paper, and an open eye. NTO had become so second nature to him, he could effortlessly slip in and out of it, utilizing only part of his attention. And this made the game quite mobile—mobile enough to take along on the plane during business trips, on the commuter train after work, in the car when driving back from the club on Saturdays, and even in the company cafeteria when stopping for a coffee in the morning or a salad at lunch.

It gave them the chance to quickly separate coworkers into the groups they understood and the groups that just didn't matter. Determining who was "regular" and who was "different" was easy because of the many factors available to consider. Austin loved the game. And now he had made it a habit for Percy. He and Percy used it as their playful revenge against their changing surroundings. And the list of employee characteristics was always growing:

1. Gender.
2. Race.
3. Ethnicity.
4. Religion.
5. Sexual orientation.
6. Accent.
7. Handicap.
8. Family social status.
9. Age.
10. Marital status.
11. Political party affiliation.
12. Rank in company.
13. National origin.

Percy felt sort of guilty about joining in with this, but, like Austin, when he was first hired at NFC, he felt that the managers at every level were just like him. As he mentioned to his wife and several other friends at the time he joined the company, "these people look like a great bunch of regular all-American guys—the kind I can get along with." He could look up the chain of command and see people who came from his same background, went to his same church, shared his same values. He could see himself in their shoes.

Everybody fit in. "They were all just like Austin's RKO people."

As Percy eventually moved up to middle level management, Austin's NTO game seemed to have even more relevance because now Percy was in the position of hiring and evaluating more employees.

Although he didn't set out to do it, he couldn't help scrutinizing people in the same way Austin had. He found himself spending an inordinate amount of time scrutinizing inconsequential characteristics of applicants to uncover who fit the "regular" mold and who would remain an outsider. And there were less and less "regular" people as time went on.

That night after dinner, Percy talked to his wife, Daisy, about his conversation with Ann.

"Percy, I can't believe you actually spoke to her like that," Daisy said as she handed the soiled dinner dishes to her husband. "It was bad enough for you to have picked through those secretaries before, but listen to what you said to Ann. She's going to think you're some mean-spirited hatemonger. And I know you're not."

Percy looked at his wife in astonishment as he shut the door to the dishwasher. "What do you mean? I don't think I sounded mean. I'm always pleasant to people—no matter what kind of background they come from. That includes strangers, too."

Percy was right. He actually *was* a pleasant person who always *did* have pleasant words for strangers—whether he passed them on the street or on the commuter train—regardless of their color, age, ethnic group, or other characteristic that made them different from him. But that was just the problem; he only felt comfortable when his interactions with these people were quick and superficial—when they were passing by or standing in line at a supermarket or train station.

Like many of the managers who had come up through the ranks of the old NFC, Percy had been raised, educated, and trained in homogeneous environments where the race, religion, gender, sexual orientation, and ethnic group of a person were easy to predict.

"And what's with that NTO game that you and Austin are always talking about on the phone?" Daisy asked Percy in mild annoyance. "I don't like how that sounds at all."

"Oh, it's nothing," Percy said with a shrug. "It's just a silly game."

"A game that makes fun of people who are different?" Daisy asked. "It's not silly. It's mean. Percy, I know you're not the kind of person who dislikes people just because they are different. So what is it? Are you afraid of them?"

"I don't know," he answered. "Maybe it's just that I don't understand them. Maybe that's it."

"But making fun of them and avoiding them isn't going to help you understand them. You'll never learn anything that way." Daisy was exasperated by Percy's inability to deal with people that fell outside his comfort zone. For years, she had noticed how much he relied on stereotypes to fill in the blanks when he first encountered someone outside his circle of friends. As a product of modern-day diversity awareness training, Percy had learned to see the diverse peoples and keep them separate from everything else that he thought was "regular."

"Everybody was a regular person like you and me . . ."

Like many organizational managers, Percy had been "victimized by diversity." Like many companies, NFC had begun to talk more and more about the importance of diversity in the workplace. Speaking about the different races, ethnic groups, religions, genders, and group distinctions that were represented in the world, the NFC honchos began to preach things such as "recognize our diversity," "value diversity," "embrace our differences." And that's exactly what Percy and others did—they paid complete attention to the differences between workers—noticing who was white and who was not, who was male and who was not, who was heterosexual and who was not. It was a game of separating people from the group.

Since the very word "diversity" comes from the Latin word *diversitas* or apart—it was no surprise that Percy's or anyone else's focus on differences would eventually break an organization into a hundred different pieces.

3

The Incident

"Mr. McGee," Ann announced while standing in the doorway. "I just got off the phone."

Percy looked up. "Yes?"

"That was the CEO's office. He would like to see you in his office at noon."

"Did they say what it's about?"

Ann leaned up against the doorsill. "I asked if it was regarding the 100th Anniversary committee work, but his assistant said it wasn't."

Percy thought for a moment. "Well, you know I'm up for review soon. It may have something to do with the Senior VP job I'm up for."

"Or," Ann suggested meekly. "It might have something to do about that incident with Austin Butler."

Percy paused near the doorway. "I hope not." He leaned up against the doorsill and thought about Butler, one of his best salesmen and closest friends. He thought back to the meeting when the "incident" first took place. It was not a pleasant memory.

Austin had been listening to some of the comments made during a gathering of his vendors at the company headquarters. The meeting was about to close when a vendor from the West Coast region stood up.

"Austin, I wanted to know if NFC plans to introduce any new flashlight models during the next 12 months."

Austin looked in Percy's direction, then nodded. "We have some new designs on the drawing board, but we're always looking for good ideas. And since you guys are closer to the customers than we are, we hope you'll give us some suggestions."

The West Coast vendor stood up. "Well, my suggestion is that you offer a lightweight leg-light flashlight."

"A leg-light?" Austin asked.

The vendor nodded to the salesmen and then looked around the table at a few of the other vendors who were also nodding in agreement. "Yeah, you know, something that kids or runners can strap to their legs for safety when they're walking or running along a dark street."

Austin scratched his chin thoughtfully. "That's an idea. A leg-light."

"Yes, I think it would be a trendy, but practical item. Young people shy away from reflector vests because they seem old-fashioned and awkward. As you know, I sell in the southern California area and I could see you launching it there and in New York. Maybe the light could blink or strobe. I could see lots of kids and teens liking that feature."

Several other vendors at the conference table seemed to like this idea as well.

Austin nodded. "Yes, I can see that. I like the image of those Beverly Hills kids and Hollywood types. That will give the product some glamour."

The vendor shook his head. "No, I'm not talking about the Beverly Hills crowd, I'm talking—"

"Oh that's even better," interrupted Austin as he imagined an even better audience. "Right, the blonde sun-and-fun beach types."

"No," the vendor finally said. "Beach kids don't need flashlights. I sell in the more populated southern part of Los Angeles."

"Now wait a second," Austin said after realizing the vendor served a consumer quite different from what Austin had considered targeting. "Remember we have a reputation to uphold. NFC is a brand with a positive image. We surely don't want to start niggerizing our products. The last thing we want is to be overaccessorizing lamps that start getting associated with hoodlums running around in South Central Los Angeles, robbing and looting from Chinese grocery stands."

Percy's mouth dropped open as the rest of the room fell nervously silent.

"What I mean," Austin continued, "is that of course we want to get those minority customers—whether they're in South Central or elsewhere, but we don't need to be making a product that will be so closely associated with them. If we do that, we might as well as just kiss our core customers good-bye. Once we start associating our products with that ghetto element, the core NFC customer will never buy our brand again. They surely don't want to purchase a product that is also clearly being used by the wrong kind of customer."

Before the vendor could respond, Percy stood up, thanked the vendors and called an end to Austin's meeting. He rushed out of the room before he could lock glances with his friend. This was not the kind of situation that Percy liked to handle. And he knew it would be best if it was ignored.

"So Mr. McGee," Ann continued. "The CEO may just want to talk to you about the things that were said at Austin's conference meeting with the vendors."

Ann's point brought Percy out of his deep thoughts. "I hope not. And even if that's what he's calling about, he shouldn't be talking to me about it because that racial stuff had nothing to do with me. That was all Austin Butler. He was the one that called those vendors together. He was the one that ran that meeting and said all those things. I'm totally clean on that one."

Ann looked into Percy's office. "Well, Austin *is* one of *your* salesmen."

4

The Three Faces of Bias

It was 12 noon when Percy was welcomed into the CEO's office.

"It is a pleasure to see you, Sir." Percy extended his hand while noticing that none of the 100th Anniversary charts or material were laid out on the conference table.

"And you, too, Percy." The CEO gestured his vice president to the chair near the couch.

Percy sensed that this might, after all, be about his promotion. It just might be the moment he'd been waiting for. His department had met more of last year's goals than any other department. With no documents indicating a 100th Anniversary planning conversation, this *had* to be about his anticipated promotion.

"I'm sure you can imagine why I called you up here?"

Shaking his head modestly, Percy suppressed a proud smile while thinking of the bottle of champagne he'd be picking up at Sam's Liquor Shop tonight. "Here it comes—Mister Senior Vice President," he thought to himself while pondering which cigars he'd use to celebrate.

"It's about Austin Butler."

Austin Butler? Percy couldn't believe his ears. Ann had been right. This *was* about the "incident."

The CEO sat down behind the desk. "And I hold you personally responsible."

Percy was shell-shocked. Austin Butler? Personally responsible? This made no sense. "Sir, I agree that Austin is one of my salesmen. But with all due respect, Sir, how can you say I'm responsible? I had nothing to do with the things he said to those vendors."

The CEO leaned back in his chair. "You mean you were surprised?"

"Of course I was," Percy responded, sounding almost convincing. "What kind of an idiot would jeopardize a half-million-dollar account with one of our best vendors like that? Blatantly telling them we didn't want our products to be associated with those kind of customers. How could I not be surprised?"

The CEO frowned. "Oh, so you mean you had no idea that this Austin was a bigot?"

"Well—Sir. I never really thought about it. I mean, all I knew—or even cared about—was his ability to sell our products and keep our vendors happy."

The CEO was not entirely satisfied. "Well, I'd never met the man until after the incident, but tell me Percy, hadn't you interviewed him and hadn't you spent any kind of time with him over the last few years?"

". . . All I knew or cared about was his ability to sell our products . . ."

Percy thought back and recalled all the lunches and golf games he'd shared with Austin. Ironically, he was the one who had persuaded Austin not to leave the company a few years back when their friends were trying to hire him away to the White Light Company. "Well, sure, I'd spent time with Butler, Sir," Percy explained. "But I never thought he'd say things like that right in people's faces. I mean that's incredibly stupid—like staring into the Pope's face and telling him you hate Catholics. Just stupid."

The CEO sat up. "Well I don't tolerate bias in my company and I'm surprised you didn't detect it in an employee that you, yourself, had hired. Narrow-mindedness of any kind is bad for NFC. And it suggests that our people are missing the bigger issues we need to be tending to as we expand this business. I thought I'd made that clear a long time ago to people."

"Well, I promise you, Sir, I have straightened out Austin, and I assure you that the others in my department have learned from his mistake. We have no other biased people in my department. I'm certain of that." Percy nodded resolutely although he had actually decided not to discuss the awkward incident with Austin or anyone else. After all, what would he say to the vendors at this point? What's done is done.

The CEO seemed skeptical. "Before you make that claim," he interrupted, "let me ask you something? Do you know what a Passive Bigot is?"

Percy thought for a moment. "No, Sir."

"Do you know what an Active Bigot is?"

Percy shook his head again.

"Then you haven't been paying attention to my speeches on "Using Proversity" or "Becoming a Progressive Manager." Have you been applying any of these concepts in your work?"

Percy vaguely remembered receiving a printed index card with these words on it, but the CEO was always routing charts and suggestions to people's offices. Yes, his ideas made sense, and yes the CEO had some great thoughts on making employees feel valued, but who could keep up with all of it? Percy knew that his job was to improve productivity among his workers, keep down his marketing expenses, and end the year without exceeding his annual budget. He didn't have time for all the CEO's speeches. Yes, he'd shown up and pretended to listen, but the charts and lessons were useless to him. His goal was to keep up with his "real job"—not the "touchy-feely" stuff.

"No, Sir. I haven't," he finally answered.

"Percy," the CEO responded. "As an important member of the 100th Anniversary Planning Team, you should know that the reason why the National Flashlight Company has survived for 99 years since our great founder developed the first product is that we are always moving forward."

The young vice president nodded, "Sure."

"Don't say 'sure,' because I don't just mean moving forward in *profitability*. I mean moving forward in our *thinking*. Not just tolerating and accepting change, but embracing and encouraging change. When you first arrived here fourteen years ago, we were falling behind in our attempt to keep up with the changing society. This is why I've spent the last ten years trying to make changes, so we can become the kind of workplace that new workers will find inviting and inspiring."

"We've got to be more open-minded about this changing workplace, the unpredictable marketplace, and the new kinds of competition and consumers that are out there these days. It's hard, but we must keep pace with these changes." The CEO

stood up. "All this requires 'Progressive Thinking'—
and the only people who can embrace Progressive
Thinking are Progressive Managers."

Percy was still thinking about Austin Butler and
the "incident." *How dare that moron throw a wrench
into my career plans and make me look bad in front of the
CEO? How could I have known that Austin would say
such bigoted things right in front of other people?* "Sure,
Sir," he added modestly as the CEO continued.

The CEO sensed Percy's discomfort but had no
idea what he was thinking. "Do you understand
what I'm saying?"

"I hear you, Sir," the young manager answered,
particularly keying in to the words "Progressive
Manager." He liked the sound of that. While he
had always appreciated the importance of moderation, he respected the CEO. And if a Progressive
Manager was good for the CEO's company, then
Percy wanted to know how to become one. "That
sounds like something we should all want to be.
How do we get to be Progressive Managers?"

"By using Proversity," answered the CEO. "Progressive Managers focus on Proversity."

"Do you mean diversity?"

"No. I mean *Proversity*. This is something very
different from diversity. And to fully grasp it, you
need to learn more about bias. But for now, let me
explain Proversity in the simplest of terms." The
CEO stood up and walked to the flipchart in the
corner of his office. "Proversity is a much more
positive and progressive concept than diversity. It

is a progressive manager's approach to doing what diversity concepts were originally intended to do, yet failed to accomplish. It's an idea I came up with after I saw the flaws in diversity strategies."

Percy leaned forward. "I don't think I understand."

"Think of Proversity as a force that goes beyond diversity. Proversity includes the deepest characteristics that tie us all together—those shared visions and values that we all have in common even if they are not obvious on the surface. While *diversity focuses on those characteristics that make each of us different*—our race, gender, religion, age, ethnicity, and so forth, *Proversity does just the opposite: it looks for what characteristics we all have in common.* Proversity gets us beyond our biases because it teaches us to move beyond superficial differences like skin color or age. Diversity divides people. Remember that the Latin root of diversity is *diversitas,* which means different or apart. Proversity links people by finding deeper characteristics that they happen to share. A focus on *Diversity* teaches us to separate and to view people at face value—by virtue of what they appear to be on the surface. I get frustrated by people who only talk about diversity—the things that make us different. We need more than that. Diversity looks only at skin color, gender, ethnic group, accent, and other superficial differences. By focusing on diversity, we never seek to understand people at a deeper level. A focus on *Proversity,* however, teaches us to look deeper and get past face value. As leaders and managers, we need to motivate, inspire, and understand our coworkers. To do this, we need to get to the soul of people. Proversity gets past face value and finds the soul of people."

The CEO paused after realizing how long he'd gone on.

But Percy seemed to be following as he jotted down notes.

"I get frustrated by people who only talk about diversity . . . we need more than that."

"But enough of that for now," said the CEO as he looked through his desk drawers. "Let's get back to Austin—and let's look at this chart that I call the Passive Bias Framework."

Percy looked down at a chart that was drawn across a sheet of paper. There were four boxes.

"This chart explains what I mean by the terms Active Bias, Passive Bias, and Progressive Thinking—and the underlying force—*Proversity*, which drives it all."

"Austin Butler is someone who is represented at the first stage of our chart."

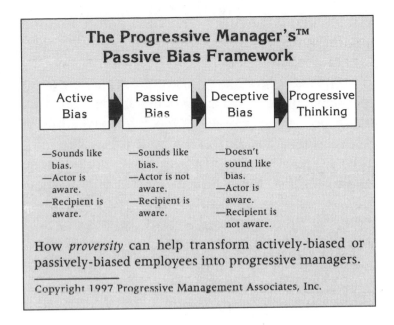

The Progressive Manager's™ Passive Bias Framework

Active Bias	Passive Bias	Deceptive Bias	Progressive Thinking
—Sounds like bias. —Actor is aware. —Recipient is aware.	—Sounds like bias. —Actor is not aware. —Recipient is aware.	—Doesn't sound like bias. —Actor is aware. —Recipient is not aware.	

How *proversity* can help transform actively-biased or passively-biased employees into progressive managers.

Copyright 1997 Progressive Management Associates, Inc.

Percy looked at the Passive Bias Framework Chart. He looked at the box on the far left labeled Active Bias.

"You see, Percy, I would call Austin Butler an Active Bigot or one who expresses Active Bias because he actively and openly displays his biased views. If he doesn't like someone of a different religion, race or ethnic group—or if he is resentful of someone with a handicap or accent—he lets them know. And this is what Austin did in that meeting with the vendors. He's the Active Bigot who yells out obnoxious names or—taken to an extreme—throws the brick, burns the cross, paints the Swastika, or makes the otherwise blatantly mean-spirited gesture." The CEO pointed to the box on the far left.

Percy nodded.

"Fortunately, most of us don't see as much of the Active Bigot as we used to. Inside the typical organization, most people are too sophisticated to be Active Bigots. They know it wouldn't be tolerated." The CEO paused. "But just because we get rid of the Austin Butlers doesn't mean there aren't a whole lot of other biased people in our organizations."

Percy dropped his eyes slightly. *What does he mean by that? The very definition of a biased person is somebody who calls people by bad names or firebombs houses or burns crosses.*

"Because you know, young man," the CEO continued while interrupting Percy's thoughts, "there are still many biased people out there who are bigots, yet they are not blatant about it. These people can be either Deceptive Bigots or Passive Bigots."

"But that really doesn't make sense," Percy interrupted. "Either a person is a bigot or he isn't. Either he *does* racist or sexist things or he *doesn't*. Why all the distinctions?"

"You've got a very narrow definition of who you'd call a bigot, Percy. One doesn't have to burn a cross or call someone a bad name to their face to be considered a biased person," said the CEO, "and that's why I talk about Deceptive Bias and Passive Bias on this diagram."

The CEO pointed to the two other boxes on the page. "You see, there are people who have no idea that they hold biased beliefs. This is Passive Bias. It's a subconscious bias that you are not even quite aware of until it's pointed out to you. Take *me* for instance."

"*You*, Sir?"

"Yes, when I was looking for a new executive assistant two years ago, I remember how my own Passive Bias came out."

"Really?"

"Percy, after personnel sent me two different male applicants for the job, I invited them into my office, acted extremely cordial, then immediately cut them from the list. They were both smart and had great experience and personalities, but something inside me said not to hire them. I didn't know what it was, but I just felt more comfortable with the female applicants—virtually all of them—even ones who seemed less qualified. I ended up hiring a woman who was less skilled simply because she made me feel more comfortable."

Percy nodded—remembering his own secretarial odyssey a while back. He'd done the exact same thing, but he sure didn't consider it a biased thing to do. "Well, Sir, I've felt the same way. You just don't expect to see or hire a man for a secretarial job."

"That's true. But why not? Why can't we get over this bias?"

"Well Sir, it may not be bigotry or bias as you call it. You know how a lot of those guys are." Percy made an unsteady gesture with his right hand. "It's just an issue of comfort. You weren't comfortable."

With his back turned to his vice president, the CEO smiled knowingly into a large picture window. "You say *'comfort'*? *That's* the first sign of Passive Bias. It's hidden behind what we call our 'comfort level.' Why wasn't I comfortable? What is so uncomfortable about a male secretary? Or a female executive, or a manager who is dark-skinned, or an employee with a foreign accent?"

"Well," Percy answered. "It's not our fault. It's just a gut response. It's not like we intend to do it."

"But that doesn't mean it's not bias—just because it's not intended. Frankly, I think it's worse because we're *not* aware of it. It's passive. Percy, think about all the problems that Passive Bias creates for a global company like this. It slows our productivity because it distracts us from our work. We end up rejecting good workers and good ideas in order to settle for what makes us feel emotionally or psychologically satisfied.

I remember when I joined my country club. I joined it because other professional guys were joining it. Then one day one of my black managers asked how he could join the club." The CEO paused.

Percy sat waiting. "And what happened, Sir?"

"Well I froze," the CEO answered. "I didn't know what to say."

"Why? Did the club have a rule that excluded blacks?"

**Three Ways That
Bias Makes Us Less
Productive**

1. We go out of our way to avoid others who are different even if it causes greater inconvenience for ourselves.
2. Instead of seeing the benefits of policies or practices that help a variety of cultures equally, we look for reasons to reject them.
3. We tell ourselves that new people and new ideas will eventually lead to our own obsolescence or loss of power and position.

The CEO shook his head. "No, we had no *written* rules against blacks joining. But like I said before, that would have been Active Bias and most people are too sophisticated to be Active Bigots. But even without the rules, I knew he'd never get in there."

"How did you know he wouldn't get in?" Percy asked.

"I just knew it. It had never occurred to me, but we all just knew what kind of people were acceptable and what kind weren't. It was just a comfort thing. People just knew not to bring a black or a Jew or whatever. You never nominated them for membership and you never brought them as guests."

Percy shrugged his shoulders with a dismissive attitude. "Well, Sir, I wouldn't be so hard on yourself. They probably wouldn't have wanted to be there anyway. They're not really golfing people. And it's not like you joined the club because it had only one kind of people. You probably joined it because it has a great golf course."

"That's what passive bias is all about. We only want people who make us feel comfortable."

The CEO did not relent as he slid down to the edge of his large mahogany desk. "That's what I tried to tell myself. I told myself that they probably wouldn't want to play golf there anyway. I told myself that I was no bigot and that I had nothing against those people. 'I'm just here for the golf and the tennis and the swimming. And I don't make the rules here.' That's what I said to myself."

"And that's right, Sir."

"No, Percy. It's not right. I was a Passive Bigot. True, I hadn't consciously said, 'Let's keep out all these different people,' but I kind of knew that it was the policy—and I kind of supported it in that I wasn't going to rock the boat and change it. I knew how much clubs helped people like us—people in the business world. They are great for building contacts, sharing information, expanding networks, and I really didn't care that we were locking out other groups. It was like our own kind of affirmative action. We didn't call it that, but that's what it was—and *is*."

Percy shrugged again. "But Sir, you *didn't* make the rules there. *You* didn't intend to hurt people."

"And that's what Passive Bias is all about. We Passive Bigots are usually not aware of what we're doing. Either we just don't know how we feel, or we forget how much the whole issue of 'comfort level' affects our actions. We want to stay around people who are like us—at any cost—because it makes us feel comfortable."

Percy nodded—not fully sure that he agreed.

The CEO picked up the chart and looked at it closely. "It's not only wrong on a moral level, but Passive Bias can hurt us on a business level as managers."

"'Deceptive Bias' is another dangerous form of bigotry," explained the CEO. "Whereas the Passive Bigot is hardly aware of his bias, the Deceptive Bigot is extremely aware of it, but decides to couch it with clever tricks—or deception. He uses politically correct terms in front of others, and then uses the real words—the mean ones—behind their backs. Like the Active Bigot, he, too, looks at people in subgroups, categories, and labels—always focusing on who's different and how they're different—color, gender, handicap, religion, age, social status—you name it. When employees are Deceptive Bigots, they can never manage others because they get lost in the minutiae. They're saying one thing, but thinking another."

Percy listened intently.

"Take this chart back to your office," the CEO added. "Think about your salesman, Austin Butler, and about the mistake I made by belonging to that discriminatory country club. And since it sounds like you didn't save the card I sent to everyone, take this and tape it to your desk. These are the four steps to becoming a Progressive Manager. They include eliminating passive bias, using Proversity, applying the 12 Commandments and addressing some other issues. We will get to all these other points a little later, but for now you

---

Four Steps to Becoming a Progressive Manager

STEP 1 Recognize—and eliminate—your Passive Bias.

STEP 2 Discover—and use—the power of Proversity.

STEP 3 Apply the Progressive Manager's 12 Commandments.

STEP 4 Expand your Universe of Organizational Contacts.

---

should focus your attention on Step 1, recognizing and eliminating your passive bias."

"Sir, I will put this in a prominent place in my office."

"And let's talk again real soon, Percy."

5

How to Kill a Company

"McGee, I haven't seen you in six years."

Percy recognized the voice, but couldn't place the face.

"Roger Straight," the man said while extending his hand. "We worked together at NFC, remember? And this is—well, you remember Jim Bright. He was with us, too."

Percy's face broke into a wide grin as he stood in the lobby and embraced the two men. "Sure, Roger and Jim. Where have you guys been all this time? I haven't seen you since you guys left NFC. What happened to you?"

"Oh, we're still in the business," said Roger. "We're over at White Light."

"Wow, that's right." Percy shook his head in awe. Although it was much smaller than NFC, White Light Manufacturing Company was one of the industry's fastest growing companies. It had been started by several former NFC executives who had grown unhappy after the CEO had begun his workplace changes at NFC. White Light was extremely profitable, and while a few of their products overlapped and competed with each other, the two companies often formed strategic alliances, with NFC focusing on large accounts and White Light selling to small mom-and-pop retailers, other small- to medium-sized accounts, and a popular door-to-door residential sales program. Strategic alliances both inside as well as outside the industry had long been an important goal of the CEO.

"So have you missed us?" asked Jim.

"It's a different place now—a really different place, Jim." Percy thought of how much things changed when the White Light-bound managers left NFC. They made up a large percentage of the guys he hung out with. They were all RKO guys. "You bet I miss you. You'd be amazed at some of the people I work with. Nothing like your folks. And I hear about those snazzy new offices you got out there in that complex out in White Haven. It's a long commute, but it sure must be nice out there."

Jim and Roger gave uneasy nods. "Yeah."

"So what are you two doing here?"

Jim and Roger looked at each other, then turned to Percy.

"Well, believe it or not, we've been having some problems at White Light," said Roger. "We dumped a ton of money into our door-to-door sales program, but it's falling flat, and your CEO was good enough to set up a troubleshooting session with some of your sales and marketing staff. It's in the conference center that you have in the building next door."

Percy was shocked. Not by the fact that the CEO was helping White Light, because the CEO often said that alliances with other growing businesses could offer mutual benefits. The CEO also made it no secret that he hoped that the White Light executives would realize that his enlightened views on diverse workers and consumers were worth implementing in their own organization. But Percy was nevertheless shocked that *he* had not been told about this session—particularly since he was vice president of domestic marketing. Was the senior vice president of Marketing managing this alone?

And even more surprising was the idea that White Light needed their help. "Problems at White Light?"

"Big problems," said Jim and Roger as the three walked toward the building.

"Well I'll walk you over to the conference center," offered Percy. "I haven't been over there in months."

Percy was astounded. *How could White Light have problems? They have all the RKO people there. They all have so much in common. They are all so likable and easy to work with. They have great new offices in White Haven, which in spite of its distance from the more populated areas, is one of the swankiest towns in the state. The executives, the workers, the surroundings are all RKO people. What would possibly be wrong with them? They do everything in moderation.*

As the three walked toward the building next door, they caught up on old times. Sammy the shoe shine man and Luigi the barber were at White Light doing shoes and hair. They had their support staff working in color-coded uniforms. They even had a separate dining room for the senior managers. It was like the old NFC had been.

"Yeah, I'll never forget my last day at NFC," said Roger. "They laid me off so they could bring in one of those affirmative action hires."

"Same thing happened to me," added Jim, with irritation in his voice. "It was a good thing White Light was getting started up by the other guys."

Percy felt both sorry for and envious of Roger and Jim. Although he had never worked on a project with them during their years at NFC, he was sure they were smart, hardworking managers who would have done good things if they'd been allowed to stay at NFC. But that was the problem with hiring all these new DKO people. You end up letting go of the very people who are good for your business. But Percy was also envious of the two men because they were working for the kind of company where Percy would have felt comfortable. Good regular guys.

"*Buenos días—cuatro.*"

Roger looked at Jim and Percy, then at the others in the elevator. "What the heck was that?"

"Good morning—fourth floor."

Several people on the elevator looked at Roger in mild annoyance as they stared up at the elevator light and speaker.

Jim hit the conference center floor—number 10—as the door closed again. "Wow, it's a talking elevator."

"*Buenos días—cinco.*"

"What language is that?" Roger snapped as the other workers looked at him. "That's not English!"

"Good morning—fifth floor."

"So Percy," teased Jim, "I see your elevators announce the floors in English and Spanish. I see things are getting even more mixed up at NFC."

Percy felt totally embarrassed and defensive in front of his White Light friends. "These are not our elevators. Our conference center just happens to be in this building. We are one of six or seven tenants."

"Well, Jim," Roger said. "We didn't get out of this place any too soon. "So tell me Percy, do your toilets flush in Swahili?"

Percy rolled his eyes and hit the button for the tenth floor. He was suddenly incensed. "That's the stupidest thing I ever heard. I have nothing to do with these elevators."

Roger continued, "Why the hell do we need to hear the floors in Spanish? This is America. Why the hell is it speaking Spanish?"

Percy shrunk back feeling a little embarrassed. "Roger, there may be people working here who don't speak English."

"Yeah and that's the problem with your company and the other people in this building," said Roger. "This *is* America, isn't it?" He lowered his voice and looked around at the half dozen employees on the elevator. "They're just taking over. Just taking over. That's why being at White Light is so much better."

"Come on, Roger. Lighten up!" Percy looked around at the blank faces. He couldn't believe what his old friend was saying in front of all these people.

"Don't hush me. There's none of them around in here. And if they are, how are they going to understand me, anyway? *I'm* speaking *English!*"

He hit the "6" button on the elevator panel.

"We're going to 10, Roger. Remember," Percy insisted, "conference rooms are on the 10th floor."

"I know where we're going, but I'm not riding on this and listening to that any more. We can take the stairs the rest of the way."

"*You* can take the stairs," said Jim.

At 6, Roger stormed out, leaving Jim and Percy to take the elevator up to their final destination. "And Jim, this is the last time we're coming to

NFC for advice. They've obviously gotten too diverse for *me!*"

As Percy sat in the conference room staring up at Jim and Roger talking to the table of two dozen NFC managers, he could feel his teeth grind in envy. *Jim and Roger have it all at White Light. Why didn't I leave when they did? Everyone gets along there. Everyone speaks the same language there. Everyone there has that good old American work ethic. They all know that the right way to run a business is with moderation.*

As he looked around the room, he realized that NFC representatives from marketing, sales, and human resources were present. *What could we be telling White Light in the area of personnel? They should be advising us on how to bring back the kinds of people we used to have at the old NFC.*

Jim was ending one of his remarks, ". . . so we could use some suggestions on the door-to-door sales issues that we just outlined."

One of the NFC sales team members raised her hand. "Well, I'm not sure I see all the complexities of the problems you just outlined, but I think your White Light Lady sales concept seems a little dated. And maybe even a little sexist, too."

"But," Roger began, "we believe that having ladies sell our light bulbs door-to-door—like some companies do with their cosmetics—is what has worked for us over the last nine years since we started the company. The White Light Lady is a good concept. It's a standard for us."

"But, it's not working," insisted the saleswoman. "You just gave us figures that demonstrated how much your profits have dropped in the door-to-door sales area."

"But we like the concept," added Jim. "An attractive woman going from house to house, visiting and establishing relationships with housewives who make the household shopping decisions. That's as all-American as you can get."

Percy nodded his head, impressed with Jim and Roger's unfaltering faith in the good ideas that had worked in the past. He liked the fact that they were wed to the old simple themes. He thought of his mother and grandmother when he listened to the story of the White Light Lady concept. His own mother had sold cosmetics to earn extra spending money when he was a child.

"Jim, I hear what you're saying," added the NFC saleswoman, "but my statistics—and I imagine yours as well—prove that the number of stay-at-home mothers and housewives is dwindling significantly. So it may be reckless for you to continue to rely on that market. Your salespeople are ringing doorbells and nobody is home because the woman who used to be there is now working at a job in an office."

A few of the managers around the table nodded in agreement.

One added, "and who says the wife does all the shopping? A large percentage of men—fathers, husbands, and single guys—do grocery shopping. And they can get their light bulbs there at the supermarket."

"And to be honest," added another NFC manager, "although you like your White Light Lady concept, it seems patronizing and sexist—and I'm saying that as a man. Why not also have male salesmen on your door-to-door campaign?"

"Well, aren't we a room full of feminists," remarked Roger with a surprisingly sarcastic smirk. "We don't want to change our White Light Lady concept."

Percy agreed. He liked the old-fashioned quality of their plan. "Folks, I'd have to agree with Roger and Jim. There's something to be said about sticking to what is tried and true, and using moderation."

Several of the NFC managers looked at each other with expressions of surprise.

"But if trends and statistics say it's not relevant and it's not working," commented the saleswoman, "why hold on to the same concept? You've got to update. Maybe you want to take some of those door-to-door people and turn them into telemarketers instead. You can cover more potential accounts in less time and with less expense by using the phone. An unanswered phone takes up less sales time than an unanswered doorbell."

Roger looked at Jim and shrugged. Neither one of them was convinced.

PART TWO

"MY NAME IS PERCY AND I AM A PASSIVE BIGOT"

6

"Is That What I Sound Like?"

When Percy got back to his office after the troubleshooting session with Roger and Jim to discuss the White Light problems, he finished reviewing the agenda for his upcoming sales meeting. He began looking over the list of new salespeople that had joined NFC this past fall. Even though he was still amazed that the White Light people were having some minor problems, it was times like this that he really envied the workforce they had assembled over there. After coming across a few names of NFC employees he couldn't pronounce, he lapsed back into his old favorite pastime.

"Now there's one," he mumbled. "And another—and there's—"

"Excuse me, Mr. McGee," Ann interrupted tentatively as she walked toward Percy's desk with a memo. "This just came from the public affairs department."

To the Staff:

As you know, NFC has been making special arrangements for the celebration of our 100th Anniversary next year. As our CEO stated, our goal is to demonstrate our Progressive Thinking in both our practices as well as our image. We are always looking for new ways to express this Progressive Thinking in our promotions and advertising.

During the last few months, we have received a wide range of suggestions. One suggestion that has come from many of our new employees has been to both change and update the company's logo (National Flashlight Company: Lighting Our Nation From Sea to Shining Sea) to better reflect our more diverse consumers and employees.

As a company that employs and sells to many beyond our nation's boundaries, it has been suggested that the logo be NFC: Lighting the World.

Let us know how you feel about this more progressive and broader concept. We feel it embraces more people and views just by altering a few words. What do you think about it?

"I think it stinks!"

Ann looked up. "I beg your pardon?"

"It stinks. Did you see this memo, Ann? This is *our* company and it's *our* country and I'll be darned if these people will come in here and make us change everything." Percy was steaming as his feet hit the floor. *This would never be an issue over at the White Light Company.* "The next thing you know, they'll be changing the name of our company to some foreign sounding name and getting rid of our American Eagle."

"What do you mean?" Ann asked. "Mr. McGee, I don't think it's so drastic. I think the CEO is just trying to be sensitive to the different types of people who buy our products and who work at the company."

Percy pounded his fist on his desk. "This is what happens when you hire all these outsiders. Ann, this place is changing. I tell you it's changing for the worse. What's with all this international 'world' stuff? This company was doing just fine when it focused on selling to plain, old Americans. Why do we have to accommodate every person who wants a job here? I remember a time when we looked out for just ourselves and we didn't have a zillion DKO people running around suggesting what we should do and how we should say things."

Ann shook her head, "Well, Mr. McGee, I think it's good to make the employees feel appreciated. You'd be surprised how just a few little changes might make people feel more comfortable."

Ann gave up when she realized Percy wasn't interested in her opinion. Even though he was offended by Roger's comments about the Spanish-speaking elevator, Percy knew nobody was around now. He could say what he wanted since nobody was going to be offended. "You give these people a chance to work here, and then they try to change everything—the holidays, the dress code, even the lunch menu. They're just taking over."

"Please, Mr. McGee," said Ann in exasperation. "Don't forget your 10:30 meeting."

Percy looked up. "What?"

"Your next meeting with the CEO is at 10:30."

"Oh shoot!" Percy exclaimed with annoyance in his voice. "Why did you let me go on like that? I forgot all about the meeting. I'll screw up my promotion."

"You're late."

"I'm sorry, Sir. I was just—"

The CEO stared out of the floor-to-ceiling picture window that looked out over the company grounds. "You were just what?" he asked. "Thinking about the chart I left with you the last time?"

"Well, not exactly."

The two men simultaneously pulled out their copies of the Passive Bias Framework.

As Percy glanced across the chart, he started thinking about his growing list of salespeople. "Don't take this the wrong way, but exactly what

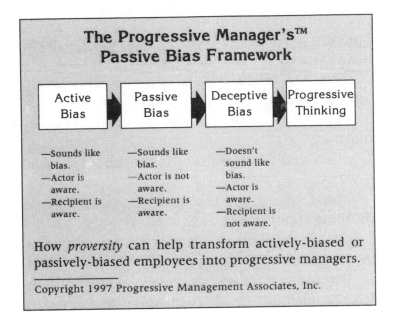

The Progressive Manager's™ Passive Bias Framework

Active Bias → Passive Bias → Deceptive Bias → Progressive Thinking

—Sounds like bias.
—Actor is aware.
—Recipient is aware.

—Sounds like bias.
—Actor is not aware.
—Recipient is aware.

—Doesn't sound like bias.
—Actor is aware.
—Recipient is not aware.

How *proversity* can help transform actively-biased or passively-biased employees into progressive managers.

Copyright 1997 Progressive Management Associates, Inc.

is so bad about being what you, Sir, are calling a Passive Bigot, especially if nobody's hurt by it, and when it's not intended to be malicious? Of course, it doesn't sound like the nicest name in the world, but what's so bad about being a Passive Bigot?" He paused and thought about the difference between himself, Austin, and Roger Straight. Roger and Austin said things in front of people that were hurtful. Percy knew that the CEO had called himself a Passive Bigot before. Percy knew he, himself, sometimes had bad feelings about people, but it certainly wasn't bigotry and he certainly never hurt anybody. He would just sometimes rant in his office by himself. "And what if you suddenly realize you're one of them, how and why do you get to Progressive Thinking? I see there's another stage on this chart. We haven't talked about it."

The CEO smiled, "Oh, so you must have gotten our memo about the logo change."

Percy was surprised. "What makes you say that?"

"Isn't that what you're thinking about?" asked the CEO.

"Well, yeah, but how did you know I was thinking about that?"

"Because I figured this new memo was going to smoke out a few Passive Bigots."

Percy sat up. He was shocked by the remark. He felt offended and he almost wanted to ask whose side the CEO was on. "Don't get me wrong. I'm not saying I'm a Passive Bigot. I was just asking, what's so wrong with *being* a Passive Bigot? Like earlier this week you said that you felt you were a Passive Bigot for belonging to a club that discriminated against different groups of people. If you didn't make the rules, why should you be held accountable? And after all, what you do on the weekend is your own business; it's got nothing to do with your job at NFC."

Percy looked over at the mirrored glass and saw his own reflection. He felt good about the point he was making. How could the CEO disagree?

"Now that's the voice of the Passive Bigot, Percy," said the man behind the desk. "Think about what you're saying. You think it's okay for me to support and belong to a discriminatory organization on the weekend and then try to govern my company and treat all my employees on a color-blind, ethnic-blind, religious-blind, and gender-blind basis during the week?"

Percy nodded. "Well, Sir, I guess so."

"Think about that. Is anyone so schizophrenic that they can be a complete bigot on the weekend at the club and then arrive at the office on a Monday morning and suddenly be open-minded and treat or evaluate everybody on an equal basis?"

Percy saw his point. "Probably not."

"That's right. I have to be consistent with my beliefs. Progressive Managers recognize that they have to set an example and that they will be judged not just by what they say in the office, but also by what they do on the weekend. If I have certain attitudes about people on the weekend, I'll have the same attitudes in the office, and that's potentially destructive."

"So, Sir—it's an issue of fairness."

"Percy, it's more than just that. There are economic reasons to explain why I feel this way. Ever since my great-grandfather started this company, we have tried to do the right thing. Of course, years ago, we didn't always accomplish that. But our even greater motivation has been our desire to grow our business and make money. Let me give you an example."

The CEO opened up the latest NFC annual report. "Percy, do you know how many countries we market our products in? Do you know where our greatest growth is? It's not through flashlights like it was when you first got here—and more importantly, our greatest expansion is not even here in this country. Do you know the changing demographics of our domestic consumers, or even of our domestic workers?"

Percy nodded nonchalantly. "Of course, but—"

"There are no 'buts.' Should we ignore the consumers in China? Should we overlook those things that will appeal to them or ignore those things that disturb them?"

"No, Sir, of course not."

"And what about the Chinese consumers who live here in America? Do we ignore their sensitivities?"

"Well—no."

The CEO continued. "And what about the Chinese-American employee who has certain sensitivities and who happens to be a great contributor to our workforce? And what if he also understands certain customers better than we do—especially when we are just starting to sell to that group?"

"Well—" Percy didn't know what to say.

The CEO pulled out a directory of four-year colleges. "Percy, look at the workforce. Look at the wide range of people who are coming out of college, training schools, graduate programs, from companies all around the world. They don't all look like you."

Percy dropped his head. *And that's part of the problem, he thought to himself. Regular kinds of people are predictable and comfortable. All these others are impossible to figure out. They look different, talk different, have different styles. Everything about them is hard to figure out.*

"But there are bottom-line reasons for accepting, embracing, and tapping into our diverse consumers and our diverse employee base. Even with the challenges against affirmative action, we can move beyond the notion of doing good simply by recognizing that all these different groups can—and are—benefiting our company."

Percy nodded. Here was the first time he had ever heard an argument that made him consider the possibility that differences might be beneficial to NFC. He had never considered the economic benefits.

The CEO continued, "Before, I told you about the other stage in the framework: 'Deceptive Bias.' Whereas the Passive Bigot is hardly aware of his bias, the Deceptive Bigot is extremely aware of it, but decides to couch it with clever tricks— or deception. When employees are Deceptive Bigots, they can never manage others because they get lost in the minutiae. They're saying one thing, but thinking another."

Percy listened intently.

"How can you lead when you are focused on everyone's differences? This is why we must do more than just recognize diversity. Yes, diversity among our consumers and workers is beneficial to our bottom line, but we can't stop there. It's not enough to notice our differences. Sometimes it is actually counterproductive if we stop there."

"As I said before, the Latin word *diversitas* means difference or contradiction. The root *di* means two or apart. In other words, diversity draws attention to what *divides* us. In a sense, a focus on diversity can keep us apart because it emphasizes what is different about each of us. How can you build teams and encourage teamwork when most of the time

---

"How can you lead when you're focused on everyone's differences?"

---

you're drawing lines between the insiders and the outsiders? How can you set an example when you think of yourself as being apart from the others? How can you motivate people and make an organization progressive when you are being either passive, deceptive, or divisive? If you simply notice the diversity and stop there, you haven't moved to the next level because you've only labeled people—and often in a divisive manner. When you're consumed with bias, you lose sight of what's important, you lose your creativity, you forget the basics. You probably even forget your appointments!"

How to Recognize Your Own Passive Bias

1. What you notice first about people around you are the characteristics that make them different from you.
2. You make it a general rule never to discuss the subjects of race, ethnicity, politics, age, religion, gender, and sexuality when you are at work.
3. When others make bigoted remarks or jokes, you either laugh or say nothing because you don't want to seem sensitive or self-righteous.
4. When you see media that is targeted at an ethnic, gender, or religious group that you do not represent, you usually ignore it.
5. When you look for a mentor or a protege, you pick someone that reminds you of yourself.
6. If someone tells you about a cultural difference of theirs (e.g., dietary restriction, religious or ethnic holiday) that you have never heard of, you rarely ask questions.
7. You are affiliated with organizations that practice subtle discrimination, but you say nothing because you didn't create the group's rules.
8. Before you hire someone for a position, you have a vague picture in your mind of what the ideal candidate would look like.

(Continued)

> ## How to Recognize Your
> ## Own Passive Bias
> ### *(Continued)*
>
> **9.** Your conversations often make use of phrases like "you people," "our kind," or "those people."
>
> **10.** You avoid talking about cultural differences when dealing with people that are different from you because you're afraid of saying the wrong thing.
>
> **11.** When complimenting someone from a different background, you might tell them, "You are nothing like the other _____s" or "I really don't think of you as a _____."
>
> **12.** There are people in your organization that you like and respect, but whom you would feel uncomfortable introducing to your family or close friends.

The young vice president smiled sheepishly.

"The Deceptive Bigot wants to hold on to his bigoted views, so he just says the right stuff so nobody will ever challenge him. Most of us harbor Passive Bias because we are ignorant or naive about how dangerous our attitudes are. The Deceptive Bigot is worse because he knows, but just doesn't care. He wants to preserve his bias."

The CEO paused and stared out the window at the great green lawn that led up to the NFC

How to Recognize Your Own Deceptive Bias

1. You are obsessed with using politically correct terms when speaking with others who are different, but you use completely different terms when those same people are not around.

2. You don't want a coworker to attend your private party because you don't want their kind in your home. But instead of admitting that you'd feel uncomfortable, you tell them they might not want to come because *they* might not feel comfortable.

3. When you're around those who are different from you, you go out of your way to use their culture-specific slang or drop references in order to make them think you embrace their background.

4. Your child has embarrassed you by using a bigoted word in front of you and the insulted party. You later tell your child that his primary mistake was letting others hear him use the word.

5. You say you're frustrated by seeing segregated lunch tables in the cafeteria, but you are secretly happy that "everyone knows their place" and that no one is trying to integrate your table. Because, after all, you wouldn't try to integrate theirs.

6. Even though you truly believe that the group you represent is superior to another, you will sometimes resort to group self-deprecation in order to convince others that you are open-minded.

reflecting pool at the front edge of the property. The NFC Eagle statue reflected brightly against the water.

Percy hated to think that he was anything like Roger at White Light. Did he really sound like Roger? He told himself that he only wanted to keep things as they were. He had nothing against anybody.

On the CEO's desk, Percy noticed two sheets of paper that talked about Passive Bias and Deceptive Bias.

"Take these sheets and think about the things all of us are guilty of when we hold biased views and forget to embrace Proversity. These sheets will help you identify your own Passive Bias and Deceptive Bias." The CEO paused, "You may even find yourself or your friends from White Light if you look close enough."

Percy felt uneasy with the thought that he might very well find what the CEO was implying.

7

A Meeting
of the Minds

"So," Ann asked, "what's this special project you're doing for the CEO?"

Percy emerged from what seemed like a deep fog. He had been studying the card now taped to his desk: "Four Steps to Becoming a Progressive Manager." "Yeah," he thought, "Step 1—Eliminating Passive Bias, then Step 2—Using Proversity . . ." As he leaned over his desk top, he felt like a million things were being thrown at him. Ann repeated herself. "What's the project?"

"Oh, I'm sorry, Ann. The CEO wants me to come up with a special marketing campaign idea that will tie into our 100th Anniversary."

"Well, you don't seem very excited. Isn't this a good opportunity for you?"

"Sure it's good—if I could do it the way I want." The vice president rolled his eyes and turned away from the card with the four steps. "But not only did the boss already pick the whole committee for this, but he says I've got to run it with Marsha Winston as my vice chair." Percy handed Ann the CEO's list of committee members.

"What, you two don't get along?"

Percy shook his head. "I barely know the woman, but I've heard enough about her to know it'll never work. She's a lateral hire who just got here two years ago from Republic Lighting Company. You know, one of those women that's just a you-know-what-on-wheels."

"So, she's not too smart?"

"Who knows if she's smart?—who cares? I just don't want to work with her. She's assistant vice president of marketing in the Northeastern region—from New York—or should I say New Yawk. You know the type: single woman from Manhattan who's too mean and aggressive to get a husband so she ends up trying to be a woman executive instead. A real ball-buster."

Ann looked farther down the list of names on the CEO's memo. "You never know. She may be good."

"I doubt it."

Percy looked over Ann's shoulder at the list of names the CEO had assigned to the 100th Anniversary Marketing Committee.

"Hmm. Calvin Jones? Wasn't he the top sales-man two years ago?"

Percy rolled his eyes again. "Yeah, and last year. But he's not the kind of person you'd put on a com-mittee to plan a high-profile campaign like this."

"Why?"

"Well, he's sort of really black—if you know what I mean."

Ann shrugged her shoulders. "What do you mean?"

"Don't get me wrong," Percy explained inno-cently. "I've got nothing against blacks. After all, he's one of our best on the salesforce. I mean that boy can sell like nobody's business, but we've al-ways had him on the inner-city accounts. So he's used to all the jive-talking types. He's not very mainstream if you know what I mean. Not the best kind of person if you're trying to come up with mainstream ideas for a national anniversary campaign."

"And who is this Karl Frank? He doesn't sound familiar."

"Well, the CEO wants to include staff outside the United States too. And Karl is director of mar-keting in Germany somewhere. I think Munich or Brussels."

The secretary thought for a moment. "I don't think you mean Brussels. I think that's in Belgium."

"Whatever. You get my point. He's one of those big, strapping blond Germans. Presentable at a public celebration, but won't be much help on the committee."

"Why do you say that?"

Percy was surprised by Ann's naivete. "First of all, he's not in the domestic office so he's only good at selling abroad. Foreign customers may be a big part of our business, but they're not the foundation or historic backbone of NFC. And like most of those Germans, Karl has absolutely no creativity at all."

Ann gave a strange nod. "Oh, so you've worked with him before."

"No," he added with a laugh, "I just happen to know what they're like. Organized and methodical as hell, but ask them to create a campaign or an original idea and they fall flat on their blond faces."

Percy walked around Ann's desk. *It's not that I'm being narrow-minded. I just have a good idea of the problems ahead. How could I ever find Proversity in a group like this? Nobody has anything in common.* "You know, the longer I look at that list, the more I realize I'm going to need Butler on this committee."

"You don't mean *Austin* Butler?" Ann was shocked.

"Sure. Just look at this group. A bunch of odd-balls that'll never be able to connect with each other. Nobody has anything in common. At least I know I can get along with Austin. He's been here almost as long as me. He understands the real NFC, and will know the kind of red, white, and blue marketing campaign that'll work. Even if the others are off on their own little tangents, at least he and I will be in synch." Percy paused. "I mean even the ones that ought to be normal—aren't. Like this one: Phillip Christianson, the Christian Christian," Percy added in mocking tones.

"Who's that?" Ann asked while looking at the memo.

"One of these preppy boarding school right-wingers. If he wasn't so damned religious, I'd swear he was gay. He sure seems gay to me. How's *he* gonna help us?"

Ann adjusted her computer keyboard.

"And Sylvia Rodriguez," Percy added. "Probably another one of those affirmative action hires. Some of these foreigners have got accents so thick you can't tell the difference between *their* English and *our* Spanish. They're enthusiastic, but who can understand them?"

Ann looked at the last three names on the list. "And what about Dan Kraner, Mark Spinelli, and Masako Akatani? You know them?"

Percy thought to himself and then chuckled. "Yeah, that Kraner's a real funny Jewish guy from New York. He's getting a little too old to take seriously, but the guy's a scream. And Spinelli is one of those community college graduates who came from one of those real working class families." Percy grimaced as he looked at the page.

"A hard worker?" Ann asked.

"I guess so, typical immigrant type. And to top it off, he's crippled." He paused. "And who's the last guy?"

"Mm, oh Akatani. Sound familiar?"

Percy grimaced again. "What is that, Chinese? I think he's from the West Coast some place. Who knows."

Ann handed the memo back to him. "And you're sure you want to add Austin Butler?"

"I'm more than sure. Looking at this bunch, I'm positive. I gotta even this group out some. Or otherwise, I'll feel like an oddball, too." He couldn't stop thinking about all the people over at the White Light Company. They'd never have to deal with situations like this.

As Percy prepared for the special anniversary marketing meeting, he pushed the NFC Eagle statue to the corner of his desk, and then looked over the agenda that Ann had typed:

**100th Anniversary NFC Marketing Plan
Strategy Meeting 1**

    I. Welcome by Chairman Percy McGee

    II. Discussion of Goals by Austin Butler

    III. Introductions by Committee Members

    IV. Scheduling of Future Meetings

    V. Setting Anniversary Marketing Budget

    VI. Marketing Used at 75th Anniversary

    VII. New Marketing Ideas to Consider

Ann stared across Percy's desk. "I reserved Conference Room 31B from 10:00 A.M. until 3:00 P.M., ordered ten lunches and am about to messenger an agenda up to the CEO's office."

Percy nodded. "That's fine."

Ann lingered. "But before I send it upstairs, are you sure you want to include that section with Austin Butler on the agenda? I mean, shouldn't Marsha's name be on there?"

"Why her?"

"Well, she is your vice chair. And Austin is not the most popular person these days."

Percy laughed. "Ann, Austin is one of my buddies. We're friends. I can't just ignore him. And plus, I didn't ask that witch to be my co-chair. Just because I have to include her on the committee doesn't mean I have to listen to her or give her any power."

"Power?"

"Right—or respect," Percy snapped. "That ballbuster can sit there like the other committee members. And that reminds me, I gotta call Austin and make sure he doesn't say anything stupid."

Just before 10:00 A.M., Percy looked at his watch and leaned over to Austin, who sat at the long conference table next to him. "Now, remember Butler, watch your mouth. I don't care what you say about this bunch when you're around me, but don't go saying anything to them that you'll regret."

A stocky, jovial-looking man in his early for-
ties, Austin leaned over and smiled. He loosened
his red necktie with a pinch of his white, starched
shirt collar. "Not sayin' a word, boss. Not a word,"
commented Austin, "But didn't I tell you that stupid Karl Frank—or should I say, Frank—enstein—
would be late? Probably in the bar across the street
putting a head on a Heineken. You know they
drink beer for breakfast where he comes from."

How's a hodge-podge group like this going to ever work together? This is a big diverse mess.

Percy stifled a laugh. "Come on. You promised.
None of those jokes during our meetings."

The group of eight all came to their seats as
Percy sat up in his chair. *Right on time, he thought
as he cleared his throat.* He was feeling confident
about himself, but still a little anxious about the
group dynamics. He looked around the room
from face to face. It was like the U.N. around that
table. He was reminded of that old saying, "What's
wrong with this picture?" It was obvious: color,
gender, race, religion, ethnic group—nobody
had anything in common. *He forged ahead and told*

himself, the CEO's gonna be watching, and I've got to deliver on this.

After Karl Frank sat down, Percy looked around the table and counted eight people besides himself. He looked down his list of names. There were ten names including his own. One person was missing, so he looked around the table again, and although he'd never met most of the people on his list, he made some mental notes.

"Can we all come to order?" As he saw Marsha moving toward the chair nearest him at the head of the table, he bent over to Austin.

"Why don't you slide over here, Austin," Percy announced loudly, "so the girls can sit together?"

Marsha frowned as Austin vacated the seat next to Sylvia Rodriguez.

"You're the boss—whatever you say." Austin gave a big smile.

Percy surveyed the room. Still one person from the sheet of names was absent. He stood up. "I want to thank all of you for assisting me on this committee. Although I haven't had the pleasure of meeting most of you before, I see one of our committee people has not arrived, and my guess is that it's—um, Masako Akatani."

Marsha looked around the room.

"Ann, get me Mr. Akatani's office," Percy shouted into the intercom on the table.

"I'm sorry, who?"

"Mr. Akatani for our committee meeting . . . Masako Akatani. He's late."

"I believe that's *Miz-z,*" interrupted Marsha.

"Well, excuse me," he said without a smile while pressing the intercom again. "Ann, I'm told that's pronounced *Mizzako* Akatani." Tell him we're waiting."

A few people laughed quietly around the table.

"Now Masako, do you feel comfortable with trying to come up with favorite American rock singers from the past if we use that in the anniversary celebration?"

"Sure."

"Because," Percy continued, "you may not have a good sense of what was truly popular here in our country versus what you got to see as a child in your own."

Masako turned her head slightly. "My own? My own *what?*"

"Your own country," Percy announced while standing at the chalkboard. "You know how the trends are—one trend may be widespread here and yet never reach the folks in China."

"China?" Masako asked while unbuttoning the cuff of her blouse.

"Oh, I'm sorry. I thought you were Chinese."

"No, I'm Japanese."

Percy grimaced slightly. He had already made the mistake of assuming that Masako was a man's name. It wasn't until she had actually walked into the room that he discovered his error in calling for *Mr.* Akatani. "My mistake. But the point I'm making is that in your country—Japan, in your case—you can't be sure that the same music would be popular in this country as well. So just be aware of that as you choose the music for the event, and try to tap into what real *Americans* were thinking."

"I *am* a real American and I think I can figure this out without too much trouble. And even if I didn't know what music was in vogue over the last 100 years, we have access to things such as a *library.*" Masako stood up abruptly and stepped toward the phone in the back of the room.

Percy stood up in astonishment and turned to Austin, then the group. "What did I say? How was I supposed to know she wasn't Chinese?"

Austin shrugged his shoulders.

Percy rushed behind Masako. "I'm sorry. I feel just terrible, but so I don't make that mistake again, how do I know whether a person is Chinese or Japanese?

"Simple, Mr. McGee. You ask them." Masako then walked out of the room.

Thrown totally off guard, Percy looked back at his committee members, who now seemed to be avoiding his eye contact altogether. He felt awful, but he was unsure of how to explain his gaffe. "Sorry, but I guess any of us could have made that mistake. So, where were we?"

Percy stood up next to the blackboard, preparing to jot down ideas offered by the remaining committee members. "So Calvin," he began, "from your perspective, what issues do you think we need to consider as we design this anniversary campaign?" *I should probably get Calvin to focus on a separate marketing program for inner-city blacks since he understands his people better than any of us. And this would mean flashlight giveaways at rap concerts, Baptist churches, and maybe some tie-ins with a malt liquor beer or cigarette brand. Some ads on the black radio stations and cross-promotions with one of the fried chicken chains.*

Calvin opened up a ledger and took a calculator from his briefcase. "Well, I ran some numbers and found that in the past, we've forgotten to . . ."

As Calvin spoke, Percy's mind drifted away from the numbers and projections that were being offered.

When the manager concluded, the others nodded in agreement with Calvin, then they looked for a response from Percy.

"Well, I don't too much like that, what do you think, Austin?"

Austin Butler looked up from his pad of paper. "I'm sorry, chief?" he asked, still adrift in his own private thoughts.

Percy repeated his response to Calvin's suggestion. "I don't like it. What do you think? I think it's too urban—if you know what I mean."

"I agree boss, too urban. It won't sell in Peoria," added Austin as he shrugged at Calvin, still not sure of what Calvin's idea had been in the first place.

Marsha raised a hand. "Percy, can I speak with you alone for a moment? Outside the conference room?" She stood up.

Percy picked up his pen. "What's on your mind, Marsha?"

Marsha nodded to her co-chair. "Just something we should discuss outside first." She smiled politely. "Just co-chair business."

"Let's not start gossiping like a couple of old hens, Marsha. If you have something to say to me, I think we should share it with the whole committee."

All heads turned to Percy.

"Don't you agree, committee people?" Percy asked.

They shrugged uncomfortably.

From Marsha's glare at Percy and Austin, it was obvious that she didn't appreciate either of their attempts to undermine her.

To avoid the contradiction that he thought might occur, Percy stood up quickly and pointed to the clock. "Why don't we break for lunch and resume on Thursday morning?"

"Well, you know what they say about them."

"They always sit together at the same table."

"How do they ever expect to assimilate?"

Percy nodded in agreement as Austin and another sales rep looked out at the numbered tables in the lunchroom. They commented on a group of employees at table number 16 in the rear. "They're always separating themselves. How are we supposed to trust them when they're always going off alone and staying by themselves?"

"Percy old boy," added Austin as he took a bite from his sandwich, "I don't know how you manage all these types. I can barely understand 'em. Just imagine what they'd do if we ever accidentally sat at their table."

"Tell me about it," agreed the other sales rep as he looked over at the table at the back—and then over at three women from the legal department sitting on stools at another table.

"And look at those three," added Percy. "I wonder what they're gossiping about."

"What else? Soap operas or snagging a husband."

Austin and Percy laughed.

"Guys," continued Percy. "Regular people are a dying breed around here. I deserve some kind of award. All these other people are complaining that they aren't accepted—then they come in the lunchroom and separate themselves." Percy thought about what the CEO had said about fostering Proversity, but he didn't see how it would apply here. "These new people aren't even trying."

Austin laughed. "Oh they're *trying* all right— probably trying to take over."

A thought suddenly came to Percy. Maybe he should be trying something, himself. *Maybe I should be taking a first step—like the kind the CEO was encouraging.* "I've gotta go. I'll see you guys at the club on Saturday." He stood up and walked to the back lunchtable.

Calvin looked up and waved. "Hey, McGee, you wanna join us?"

The four other lunch companions looked up and made space.

"No-no," Percy insisted. "I just want to know what you folks are up to. What are you plotting over here at this table?"

The other diners looked at Calvin in confusion.

"Plotting? What do you mean?"

Percy laughed. "Oh come on. You guys always sit over here alone. The same group every day. So what's going on—some kind of overthrow?"

Calvin laughed uncomfortably. "Percy, you must be joking."

"Well—only a little." Percy smiled and then pressed on. "In all seriousness, you must admit that you guys separate yourselves from everybody else—eating at the same table every day and with the same people."

"Did it ever occur to you that you eat at the same table every day—with the same people?" Calvin sat waiting for an answer.

"And just because we don't look like you," one of the men added, "you think we have some plot in place? That's just stupid."

Percy backed away. "Forget it—forget it. Sorry I said anything." *Well you can't say I didn't try. The CEO said I should try to move beyond our differences, but look what happens. These people are impossible. You reach out to them and they bite your head off.*

"Don't you think you came on too strong?" Percy's wife, Daisy, asked him after he got home and told her what had happened in the cafeteria that afternoon.

"What do you mean, 'too strong'? The CEO said I should try to reach out to different people, and that's what I was doing. I really wanted to be friendly." The young manager felt awful. He really had hoped to make a connection with Calvin and the others at table number 16.

"Well, Percy, you never should have walked over and accused them of plotting something just because they always sit together. You'd be insulted if somebody said you, Austin, and all the other guys that sit together were plotting a takeover or conspiring to commit some group act."

Percy nodded at Daisy and saw her point. "So I guess you're saying I shouldn't give up yet?"

"Not only shouldn't you give up, but you should apologize and then start all over," Daisy said as she leaned over to set the clock on her nightstand. "If they were making room for you at their table, you should have sat down and talked to them like you'd talk to any other colleagues."

Percy switched off his light and was resolved to do a better job next time. He'd made lots of mistakes, but he didn't want to let the CEO down.

8

The Face Value of Diversity

"You asked to see me, Sir?"

The CEO offered a handshake and gestured to the couch.

Percy smiled, "We really made great headway at our first meeting. I guess you saw the agenda?" *I can't believe I'm actually saying this. We made no headway at all.*

"I did, Percy. You've got a real cross-section of people there."

"You're not kidding," Percy answered. He knew the first meeting was a disaster, but how could he tell that to the CEO? Given what had already happened, Percy felt this whole exercise could soon blow up in his face. It had become totally clear to Percy how his own passive bias had gotten in his way. He'd never thought of himself as being a bigot, but he now saw how much havoc he had created with his remarks, even though he'd never intended to hurt anyone's feelings. He knew it was time to put his NTO game to rest. It now occurred to him that he did not know how to manage a diverse group of people—all of them with nothing in common. Masako had walked out, Calvin felt he was being ignored, Marsha said she was being undermined. This was a big setback if he had any hopes of getting that promotion, but Percy was totally exasperated by what was going on. "Yeah," he finally said. "Everybody has a completely *different* perspective."

The CEO nodded. "And I hope you are using the power of Proversity to bring everything and everybody together."

"Yes, I know you talked about Proversity before, Sir."

"Right, Percy. If you remember, Proversity is the force that brings together people from different backgrounds and finds those common interests and goals that they all share." The CEO gestured confidently as he spoke. "I had a feeling you didn't digest all of this when we last met, but let's try it again. In the past, many organizations talked only about *diversity.* Diversity puts the focus on what makes each of us different from the other. So, for example, when the nonprogressive managers looked at a team or committee like yours, they would see a Hispanic woman, German white man, black Southern man, unmarried woman from New York, old Jewish man, a disabled man, and so forth. They put the accent on diversity—the characteristics that make all the coworkers different from each other."

Percy looked down at his list of committee members. He was eager to fix the mistakes he had made, and he was hoping that the CEO would lead him in the right direction.

"Proversity gets to the soul of people."

"And that is why," continued the CEO, "they can't build effective teams. No one is working together. This is one of the problems that's plaguing the managers at White Light. They should not be drawing boxes around different workers. They should be determining what they all have in common and finding the force or energy that will move the entire group forward. That force is found in the *Proversity* of the group: those common characteristics that are shared by people who come from very different backgrounds. Proversity gets to the soul of people. It gets you to understand people beyond just 'face value'. To inspire coworkers, we must reach in and touch their souls."

"So," Percy asked, "What is the Proversity that we find in a group like this that I am co-chairing?

Because to tell you the truth, I don't know how to manage these people. All I see are our differences."

"I'm not surprised that all you see are the differences, Percy. You've only been focusing on *diversity.* Have a seat," explained the CEO as he walked over to the flipchart on the far wall. "Let me put a couple of diagrams on this board and show you why you need to change your focus if you want to get more from your co-workers."

Percy was eager to understand this. He was also eager to understand why the CEO felt that White Light's problems were related to bias. *The group is so homogeneous over there, who would they have to be biased against? And the problems at White Light were pretty minor anyway.* "Thanks, Sir, because it seems like no matter how hard I try, no matter what I say, I keep offending these people." He was clearly exasperated and willing to take whatever help he could get. "I never have this problem with other people."

"Let's look at how your focus on diversity is getting in the way of your ability to manage people," said the CEO. "To begin with, let's think of the factors that we must consider when we hire an employee or assemble a team. What do we really want to know about these people?"

Percy stared up at the flipchart.

"There are several things that any manager wants to know about someone he is bringing into the workplace or adding to a project team. What are they?" The CEO picked up the marker and walked to the right end of the flipchart.

"I suppose," Percy answered, "we want to know if they are hard working."

"Right. Let's call that the employee's 'Work Ethic.' And that will be first in our list of Workplace Qualities that we look for." The CEO then wrote the two words on the right side of the chart. "Now what else do we want to get a sense of?"

"Maybe their ambition."

"Exactly. The CEO continued to write until he and Percy had identified 11 Workplace Qualities to look for in every employee. They were:

1. Work ethic.
2. Ambition/Energy level.
3. Knowledge.
4. Creativity.
5. Motivation.
6. Sincerity.
7. Outlook.
8. Collegiality/Collaborativeness.
9. Curiosity.
10. Judgment/Maturity.
11. Integrity.

Percy studied the board. "Well I understand why we'd want to get a sense of the employee's knowledge, creativity, motivation, sincerity, judgment, and integrity, but points 7, 8, and 9 don't seem so crucial. What do you mean by "outlook"?

"Think of it this way," explained the CEO as he looked out the window to the reflecting pond below. "Don't you want to know whether you're hiring an optimist or a pessimist? We want to employ people who have a positive outlook—people that think they really can get the job done."

"And collegiality or collaborativeness?"

"Percy, think about that. We want people who not only get their own work done, but who also excel in working with others. We want team players—coworkers who collaborate." The CEO then began looking through a stack of sheets on his desk.

"And I guess," Percy began, "we are looking for curiosity in a coworker because we want employees who ask questions."

"Exactly. We don't want people who are afraid to ask how they can improve on what they've done in the past. Inquisitive people push us all to the next level." The CEO looked up once he found the two sheets he'd been looking for. "Now if we can agree that these 11 Workplace Qualities are the primary concerns we need to address when incorporating a new person into a workplace situation, let's ask ourselves if a focus on diversity can really help us determine if employees satisfy these 11 concerns."

Percy reached for the diagram that the CEO held out. It was labeled "The 5-Step Diversity Paradigm."

The 5-Step Diversity Paradigm

| 1. Focusing on DIVER-SITY Characteristics | 2. Offers No Real Information on Work Potential and No Questions Are Asked | 3. Invites Stereotyping and Projecting | 4. Creates Incorrect Judgments, Generalizations, and Insults | 5. Creates False Personas to Hang Further Stereotypes On |

—Race.
—Gender.
—Color.
—Ethnicity.
—Religion.
—National origin.
—Sexual orientation.
—Disability status.
—Age.

—Negative stereotypes: Lazy, pushy, disagreeable, mean, stiff, unintelligent.
—Positive stereotypes: Smart, punctual, organized, fair, assertive.

Copyright 1997 Progressive Management Associates, Inc.

"Let me show you how a focus on diversity, alone, fails to help us find employees who satisfy the 11 concerns," explained the CEO. "Remember that diversity focuses on nine characteristics: race, gender, color, ethnicity, religion, national origin, sexual orientation, disability status, and age. These are the typical Diversity Characteristics that most companies and governmental agencies rely on in order to build and judge their varied workforce."

"That's true," Percy admitted. *He thought to himself—yeah. Blacks and whites, women and men, Hispanics, Asians, Italians, Irish, Christians, Jews, Muslims, Buddhists, Americans, non-Americans, heterosexuals, homosexuals, handicapped and nonhandicapped, young people, old people, yeah that's the mix.*

Nine Employee Diversity Characteristics

1. Race.
2. Gender.
3. Color.
4. Ethnicity.
5. Religion.
6. National origin.
7. Sexual orientation.
8. Disability status.
9. Age.

"The problem, Percy, is that none of these diversity characteristics can tell us anything about someone's work ethic, ambition, creativity, and so on."

"Really?" Percy asked. *What is he talking about? Most whites work hard, and many blacks don't. Most gays are creative, Asians aren't. Men are ambitious, married women aren't—*

"Unless we rely on stereotypes," the CEO added pointedly "which are never exact. And you'll see what happens when you look at the 5-Step Diversity Paradigm.

You'll see how it gets us into trouble when we focus only on Diversity Characteristics.

The CEO pointed to the third box. "We develop stereotypes in our minds and no matter how talented or ideal the worker might be, we have already decided to hang a stereotype around his neck. And whether the stereotype is a negative one or a positive one, it creates false expectations."

"I guess I know the problems of a negative stereotype being hung onto somebody," added Percy, "but what's the downside of assigning a positive stereotype? What if I stereotype someone as being smart or organized or efficient even if they aren't? It's not like they are going to get offended or be upset with me."

"Good question. But besides it not being fair to the others when you make a lot of positive assumptions about one particular person, there is an immediate flaw in your system for evaluation. If you presume that Person A is going to be superb in his communication skills and he ends up being just a little better than mediocre, your eventual disappointment in him will tell Person A that he is a total failure—when, in fact, he is about as good as the other people around him. Stereotypes create gaps between expectations and reality, and that can destroy a worker's and a team's morale."

Percy then looked at the fourth box on the 5-Step Diversity Paradigm chart. *So stereotypes lead to insults and incorrect judgments about people—like the way I insulted Masako, ignored Calvin, and assumed that Karl was a drinker.*

"And as you can see," continued the CEO as he pointed to the fifth box, "you end up with a whole lot of false personas to hang more stereotypes onto. We haven't gotten anywhere toward finding out if a worker is good for the job. This is why focusing on Diversity can be too limiting. Race, gender, religion, and those other characteristics don't give us the kind of information we need. They instead create distractions and disabling baggage."

Percy was beginning to understand his boss' point. He looked at the other chart in his hand.

"So that's why Proversity works better than Diversity?"

"Exactly," said the CEO, "but we'll talk about that tomorrow. That's explained on the other chart, and as you'll see, the Proversity Paradigm chart has six steps instead of five. In the meantime, try to apply today's lesson the next time you find yourself or others passing judgment on coworkers merely because of our focus on these superficial Diversity differences. If you don't truly embrace the Proversity of all your staff members, you will eventually create an environment where a single loose cannon will erode everything you've worked for."

9

Hostile Territory

It was a lot for him to grasp, but Percy felt that his conversations with the CEO were getting him closer to becoming the kind of Progressive Manager that the CEO wanted him to be. He now had a sense for how much his own passive bias had affected his judgment. All his life he had thought of himself as open-minded and unbiased, but now he saw how his subconscious biases could still affect those around him.

He knew there was still room for improvement, but he felt he was doing pretty well. The only area he really continued to turn a blind eye to was his troublesome friend, Austin Butler.

It was one thing to alter his own behavior, but he felt awkward about dictating to his friend. *And after all, even if Austin is a problem, he is* my *problem.*

And I'll eventually whip him into shape before any real trouble happens.

Unfortunately, by the time Percy got to his office that morning, "real trouble" had already arrived. Taped to his computer terminal was an envelope with a typed note inside.

Dear Mr. McGee:

This is a very difficult letter for me to write, but I thought you should hear it from me first—before you are contacted by anyone else.

I have enjoyed working for you over the last five years, and I think you have been very kind to me, but I recently asked our Secretarial Services office to transfer me to a new assignment.

Please do not be offended by my request, because although we work extremely well together, extenuating circumstances demand that I seek an assignment to work for someone else.

I know this is a particularly awkward time for me to request a move because of your 100th Anniversary Celebration planning, but I think it may be best for everyone if I move quickly and do so very quietly.

Yours truly,

Ann

Percy couldn't believe his eyes. Ann wanted to work for somebody else? Why? What did she mean by "extenuating circumstances," "best for everyone," "very quietly"? What was she talking about? The office had worked like a well-oiled machine since he had found Ann. Even when everything outside the office was falling apart, he knew he could count on her to keep things running smoothly and on schedule. She anticipated problems before they blew up, she kept bothersome people away when he was busy. She even knew when to offer advice on issues that went beyond her secretarial duties. She was his right hand.

All his life he thought of himself as open-minded and unbiased, but now he saw his subconscious bias affect those around him.

"Is this Secretarial Services?" Percy whispered into the phone after closing his office door.

"Yes, this is the Secretarial Services Director, Ms. Appleton speaking. Who's calling?"

Percy swallowed hard and continued, "This is Percy McGee calling, and it has come to my attention that my secretary of five years, Ann, is being transferred to work with another manager. And I'd like to know why."

There was a long pause on the other end.

"You said this is Mr. McGee?"

"That's right. Why are you moving my secretary? We work very well together."

"Well," began Ms. Appleton. "We promised Ann not to let this become messy, but she felt compelled to ask for the move. And she didn't want to be penalized for making this request, so with all due respect, I'd rather not discuss her complaint."

"Complaint?" Percy quickly searched his memory, wondering what he could have done or said to Ann that would have elicited a complaint from her. He thought Ann was the greatest possible secretary.

"Nothing is going down on paper, Mr. McGee. We're in agreement with Ann that the gravity of the situation demands that she be moved. It's best for her own piece of mind and for NFC's liability."

Liability? The more Percy asked, the more rattled he got. "Maybe I should talk to Ann, myself, because I'm totally confused."

Ms. Appleton agreed. "Perhaps you should, but please do not press her if she is unwilling to discuss it. Our lawyers tell us that in situations like this, it is best to avoid any form of further harassment. She's a good worker."

Lawyers? Further harassment? Situations like this? How could they be using these words and talking about Ann? He'd never done anything to Ann. There must be some mistake. He was so dumbstruck, he had nothing more to say to Ms. Appleton.

"Thank you for calling, Mr. McGee," Ms. Appleton added as Percy put the receiver down.

After a half hour of reviewing the last six months on his calendar, Percy was a wreck. He couldn't remember saying or doing anything during the last half year that could have elicited such a response from Ann and the Secretarial Services department. He felt awful for Ann and he felt awful about what this would mean for his own record.

He reached for the intercom button. "Ann, can I see you for a moment?"

As the secretary sat down on a chair opposite Percy's desk, she held a pad out in her hand, poised for dictation.

"No, Ann. I need to talk." He sat down in his chair and braced himself. "What's wrong? What have I done? I got your note, then spoke to Secretarial Services and they told me how serious your transfer was."

Ann dropped her head and looked down. "If you don't mind, I'd rather not talk about it. I really didn't mean to cause you any problems."

"You're not causing me any problems. Just talk to me." Percy leaned forward in his chair with a face full of angst. "I know I've been very distracted lately since I started working on the 100th Anniversary project and I am sorry if I've done something to offend you."

Ann lifted her head slightly. "I really didn't want to create a mess here, Mr. McGee. I wanted to leave quietly."

Percy was still not satisfied. "Look, I won't take it any further than here. I care about you, Ann, as a professional and as a friend. I've always intended to treat you with the greatest respect."

The secretary looked up when she heard the word "respect." "Do you really mean that?" she asked.

"Of course. Just tell me why you want to leave this job. Just tell me what I did. Please."

The secretary fidgeted with her notebook and looked down at her hands.

"Ann—please tell me what I did."

"Nothing, Mr. McGee."

Percy thought he had misunderstood her at first. "What?"

"Nothing," she responded. "You did nothing."

"What do you mean, nothing? Secretarial Services said something about harassment and lawyers and all kinds of other things."

"Do you swear you won't discuss this with anybody?" Ann asked as she got up and paced toward the window.

"Yes, of course I swear."

"Because it has to do with Austin Butler," she snapped nervously. "It's him."

Percy shook his head and braced himself to hear what his friend, Austin, had done. "What did Butler do?"

"Well, I feel very uncomfortable repeating this because I want people to take me seriously as a professional here. I know he's your friend and everything, but I heard him telling you how un-married secretaries were an easy mark and that you ought to start trying to score with me before somebody else in the office did."

Percy was shocked. He remembered that con-versation quite clearly, but he'd had no idea that Ann had heard it, too. Austin was always walking into his office saying provocative and offensive things without closing the door or seeing who was around. That was the difference between him and Austin. Austin never hid his offensive remarks or jokes behind closed doors. Austin had no discretion at all. And worst of all, Austin saw women as sex objects and not as professionals who should be taken seriously.

"Oh, he's just a crude guy," Percy answered while trying to lessen the tension in his voice.

"But you laughed when he said it—and I re-member you saying something like 'I'm taking things slow.' Then you closed the door and I went back to my work." Ann looked out the window as she spoke.

Percy stared down at his hands and felt just awful. "Ann, you know I would never do any-thing like that. I'm happily married and so is Austin. It was a terrible slip of the tongue. He was wrong and so was I. I'm so sorry, but we made a terrible mistake."

"And then two weeks ago," Ann continued nervously, "I heard you talking to him when your speaker phone was on. And he said, 'So have you broken Ann in, or am I going to have to do it?' "

Percy felt his chest sink in.

"And all you did was laugh and then take him off the speaker phone," she added.

Percy remembered the conversation vividly and hadn't even realized how awful it sounded until now. For years and years, his old friends at NFC and those over at White Light talked like that, but it was all in fun. Just guys talking. He almost never made crude, sexist remarks like that, and he felt terrible for having laughed at them. He was a laugher—not a teller—but it obviously made no difference to Ann right now.

"So, Mr. McGee, it's not what you said or did," Ann explained, "it's sort of what you *didn't* say or do. With all the women working around here these days, he must know how many of us don't like to be talked about in that way. You must know that those remarks are more than just harassing. They make it hard for me to work and to be taken seriously here. But I know Austin is your friend and if he—"

"Ann, please," Percy begged. "Please don't think of me that way. I would never say or try such things and I am ashamed that Austin would. I was wrong to laugh."

Ann wasn't convinced. "But how can either of you take me seriously as a professional if I'm seen as some sort of sex object? And if he's your friend, I know that the two of you probably—"

Percy was devastated by her tone. He could see why Ann was scared and upset with her situation. If he had a close buddy like Austin, what would make her think that he—Percy—operated any differently? Percy was seeing Austin destroy his whole friendship and working relationship with Ann. Until that moment, it had never really occurred to Percy that Austin's sexist remarks and sexist behavior added up to blatant job discrimination.

"And then when Austin asked me out last weekend, I realized his being married meant nothing. I was so embarrassed and then I realized that you might eventually put me in the same uncomfortable—"

"Ann, Ann, Ann. I'm so sorry." Percy got up from his desk, put his palm against his forehead and sighed. "I am so sorry. I've been a total coward about everything. Everything."

As the secretary walked out of the office, Percy could practically see his world crashing down on him. The Anniversary Committee, the CEO, Austin, and now Ann. Nothing he'd done so far had brought people any closer. Daisy had been right when she told him that he would eventually pay for the divisive games and conversations that he shared with Austin.

It had taken a long time, but Percy was finally realizing how much he had to do to live up to the

CEO's goal of creating a working environment that gave everyone equal respect. He wanted to be a Progressive Manager, and he was going to work harder at getting there before his chances were gone forever.

PART THREE

IMPLEMENTING
THE POWER
OF
PROVERSITY

10

Hard Lessons

The next morning, Percy was sitting at another White Light troubleshooting session and still reeling over his embarrassing conversation with Ann. He'd been able to talk her into giving him at least two weeks to make some changes. He was hoping that during that time, he could prove to her that he shouldn't be judged by the company he kept. He knew that she was right to have pointed the blame at him. What kind of manager would allow people like Austin to carry on the way he did? He knew that the CEO's Progressive Manager certainly wouldn't have tolerated it.

"We want to thank you for helping us out on these issues," explained Roger Straight. He and Jim Bright had returned for the last of two troubleshooting sessions.

This had been a miserable week. Percy was in desperate need of some upbeat news. Although he had been slow about addressing his own passive bias and about embracing Proversity, he was glad that Roger and Jim were eager to learn before they suffered what he was facing. They had spent the first session discussing the failings of the White Light Lady concept, the idea of expanding their salesforce to include a greater diversity of racial and ethnic groups, the notion of selling beyond their mostly white and affluent communities, and developing a mailer that could be translated into Spanish, Italian, and Chinese to reach segments of the population that were nearby and didn't have access to the company's mail order products because of a language barrier.

"Well we've pretty much decided to reject your suggestions on translating any of our sales material," said Roger as he looked around the room of NFC managers. "We hear what you're saying, but we like to think of our label as an all-American one, and if we started translating our sales material, it makes the core customer feel as though these foreigners are just as important."

One of the NFC salesmen raised his hand. "I can't believe you're saying that. First of all, these people are not foreigners, English is simply not their native language. Second, why would you pass up large groups of new customers when it is so inexpensive to translate your mailing material?"

Percy couldn't believe his ears. The NFC research staff had already shown that White Light's residential sales would increase by 20 percent if they were able to reach this new market of non-English speaking people.

Jim Bright stepped in to explain other points, ". . . and while we thought of the idea of sending salespeople to, or having telemarketers call on, those more racially mixed neighborhoods, we realized we would need a racially mixed staff to do the calling and visiting."

"And?" a NFC salesperson asked.

"Well, you know White Light," answered Roger with a hint of indignation. "We don't have people like that on our staff."

"Then go hire them," the salesperson snapped.

Roger and Jim stood firmly. "White Light is not ready for that type of hire."

Percy was incredulous as he listened to the blatant shortsightedness of the White Light managers.

"That's so bigoted and elitist," someone said, "and economically foolish."

"At White Light, we like to act with moderation," answered Roger. The two went on to discuss that although profits continued to plummet, they were hopeful that the White Light Lady sales method would still appeal to housewives.

Percy could see that he'd been totally wrong about White Light. Maybe those "regular" guys over there were as narrow-minded as the CEO said. If they didn't wake up soon, they'd screw up like he'd screwed up with Ann and the anniversary committee.

The next afternoon, Percy found himself at the Greenlawn Country Club with his friend, Austin Butler.

"You know, I've been thinking," Percy began as he and Austin walked away from the third hole and back toward the golf cart.

"About what?"

Percy dropped his putter into his golf bag and shrugged. "I don't know, but what if I brought Calvin, Chris, and Marsha out here to the club?"

"Is this some kind of riddle?"

Austin Butler and Percy had been members of the Greenlawn Country Club for over ten years. Percy had been nominated by a senior vice president in strategic planning, and two years later he had brought Austin in. In fact, Austin had built up his customer base through several contacts he'd made at Greenlawn.

Percy leaned up against his golf bag. "Come on Butler, I'm serious. It might improve relations between people on the committee if we got together outside the office in a place that they thought seemed special. I want them to know that I take all of this very seriously."

"Then take'em to a restaurant—not here."

"But think about it, Butler," Percy explained. "This is a nice atmosphere that will set a more positive tone for our work. And plus, they all know we play golf and do a lot of networking here. I don't want to seem like I'm hiding something from them. You know what I mean?"

"What you mean is that you're going soft, McGee. You've been listening too much to that CEO and all his Progressive Manager stuff. First of all, people here are not going to want those types around. Second of all, they are doing just fine without contacts from Greenlawn." Austin was adamant as he dropped the putter back into his golf bag and then reached into a canvas duffel bag for a towel and a bottle of water. "If you bring them here, then they'll start asking if they can join. And then what will you do? Even if a miracle happened and one of them got in, they'd make you look bad in front of all the other members."

Percy gave him a blank stare, then dug the heel of his shoe into the green.

"Oh no," Austin snapped. "I don't like the way you're acting. They'd never fit in here. And they don't need this place in order to succeed at work. They do just fine on their own."

Percy thought about the diversity stereotyping that the CEO had described in their meeting. Austin really did rely on stereotypes and it affected the whole way he judged people.

"Just imagine how they'd behave in a place like this. Percy, it wouldn't work at all."

Percy began lifting the two golf bags and the cotton duffel bag with the towels and bottles of water off the cart. He was thinking about how he could demonstrate the CEO's point.

"What are you doing?"

"Just hang on a sec—"

Austin rolled his eyes and put his towel in his back pocket.

"The boss says that stereotyping adds a burden to people and makes it hard for them to do their job and it makes it hard for their teammates to do theirs." Percy paused before continuing his point. "He says stereotypes get hung onto people like excess baggage and it slows them down, even if the victim doesn't believe or accept the stereotype. He gets slowed down just because everyone else puts it there and believes it's there."

"McGee, can we drop this?"

"Just bear with me. Let's pretend we were walking the course without a golf cart and had to carry our bags and were playing against two other guys." Percy smiled. "Let's say that you and I were Team A and the other two were Team B."

"Okay."

"And imagine that I have a whole bunch of stereotypes in my mind for people like you. Let's say you weren't Austin Butler, but you were—let's say Sylvia Rodriguez." Percy paused, "What comes to mind?"

"Hispanic woman in marketing," answered Austin.

Percy knew exactly what stereotypes Austin applied to different groups so he went ahead. "Now I realize you've never worked with Sylvia and don't know much about her, but when you think of 'Hispanic woman' what then comes to mind?"

"Stereotypes get hung onto people like excess baggage . . ."

Austin laughed. "Lazy, disagreeable, not too smart, loud, and probably—"

"Okay, okay." *Gosh, Austin really believes this stuff. I know I used to joke about it with him, but I never took it that seriously. It's like the CEO said—Butler really is an Active Bigot. He had offended and scared Ann with his sexist remarks and come-ons. He never draws a line. He doesn't hide or hold back anything. He has a specific label for every type of person.* "So think of each bag as representing a stereotype that we're going to hang onto the Hispanic woman, and let's hang it onto a Hispanic woman that we know for sure is smart, hardworking, and easy to work with." Percy picked up one of the golf bags.

"What are you doing?" Austin asked as Percy put one of the golf bags on Austin's left shoulder.

"This is called Stereotype Baggaging—and this bag represents the view that although you're on my team, you are probably not too smart." Percy then picked up the second golf bag and put in on Austin's right shoulder.

"And which stereotype label is *this* for?" Austin asked sarcastically as he held onto the second bag of clubs.

"That's the bag that represents the 'laziness' label that we have hung on you."

Austin walked a few steps. "Now I suppose this was to prove that by hanging these stereotypes on me, I won't be able to function well?"

Percy nodded as he walked in front of Austin with the duffle bag that held their towels and water bottles.

"Well," Austin answered with a couple of heavy breaths, "I'm still functioning. I'm walking right behind you."

"Oh, and I forgot—what's the third point you made before?" Percy asked with a grin. "Oh, yeah, you said she's probably disagreeable." Percy then took the third bag and dropped it into Austin's barely open arms. "Your third stereotype to hang onto. Now let's keep up so our team doesn't fall behind the other team."

With that, Austin moved six more steps to the next hole then collapsed head first onto the ground!

As Percy walked on slowly he continued, "so you see Austin, as the CEO says, the more we burden our coworkers and teammates with these stereotypes, the more baggage we're forcing them to carry. Even if they don't accept the stereotypes themselves, they are still being victimized because *we* believe in the stereotypes. And that, alone, is enough to slow them down and then slow the whole team down. Our expectations weigh people down if we refuse to see them for who they really are and what they can really do."

11

The Soul of Proversity

Percy chuckled to himself as he thought of how hard Daisy had laughed when he told her about the golf game with Austin Butler. He still hadn't confronted him about the comments he had made around Ann, but he was thinking of a way to deal with that before too long. When he arrived at the CEO's office, he saw that the eleven Workplace Qualities were still written on the blackboard.

A voice bellowed outside of the CEO's office, "And tell them that I want to do something about that cafeteria situation, too."

Percy sat up and pulled out his diagram of the 6-Step Proversity Paradigm as the CEO walked in and took off his jacket.

Eleven Workplace Qualities

1. Work ethic.
2. Ambition/Energy level.
3. Knowledge.
4. Creativity.
5. Motivation.
6. Sincerity.
7. Outlook.
8. Collegiality/Collaborativeness.
9. Curiosity.
10. Judgment/Maturity.
11. Integrity.

"Percy, I suppose you see that I left up the list from our last talk. We used the 5-step diagram and spoke about how a focus on an Employee's Diversity Characteristics—characteristics like race, gender, and ethnicity will never teach us what we need to know about the workers we hire and manage." The CEO sat on the edge of his desk and added, "But let's look at this next diagram—a 6-step diagram to note how a focus on Proversity can lead us to draw honest and constructive conclusions about these coworkers. Let me show you how we, as Progressive Managers, can focus on seven simple areas that I call an 'Employee's

---

**Six Employee
PROVERSITY
Characteristics**

1. Personality.
2. Interests.
3. Skills.
4. Aspirations.
5. Experiences.
6. Education.

Proversity Characteristics' and ultimately learn what we need to know about employees."

"As opposed to focusing on race, gender, color, ethnicity, religion, national origin, sexual orientation, disability status, and age, I believe we should first look, instead, at a worker's personality, interests, skills, aspirations, experiences, and education."

Percy nodded and the CEO continued.

"When we focus on these characteristics and how they relate to the worker we're analyzing, questions immediately come to mind. I believe this is what will get us started toward finding the right kind of employees for our organization." The CEO could hardly contain his enthusiasm. "These are all questions that we should legitimately want to raise when choosing an employee. For example, Percy, think about the questions that arise when you think of our first Proversity characteristic—

personality. What would you ask the employee if you were trying to judge his or her personality?"

Percy thought about what he wanted to know about Hector Cortez before he hired him as his newest assistant director of marketing in the Southwest region. "Well, I'd like to know about the person's sense of humor. That would tell me something about his personality. I'd also ask if he is shy or gregarious, and maybe find out what things make him fearful or uncomfortable."

"Okay, that would probably require asking at least a half dozen questions of the person to get a sense of his personality." The CEO continued, "Now how would you learn about the second Proversity characteristic—interests? What would you ask about?"

Percy stared at the second box of the chart. "I'd ask him about his hobbies, what he likes to read, maybe ask about where he likes to vacation, what sports he plays or likes to watch."

The CEO nodded. "Yes, you might ask him who his heroes are, who he admires, what musical or dramatic performers he prefers, and what kind of TV shows or movies he watches. You may even get into political heroes."

As Percy thought back, he remembered how much he had in common with Hector, but he didn't actually discover it until his second month on the job. *Yeah, that's right. We both like old John Wayne movies and we both had spent our childhood summers on claustrophobic family driving vacations (Hector in Texas*

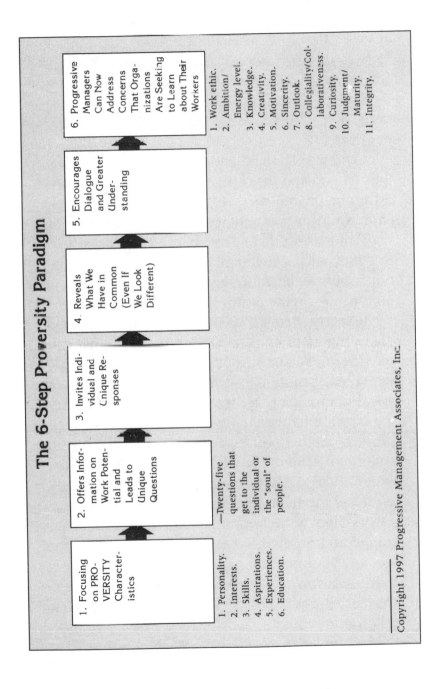

The 6-Step Proversity Paradigm

1. Focusing on PRO-VERSITY Characteristics

→ 2. Offers Information on Work Potential and Leads to Unique Questions

→ 3. Invites Individual and Unique Responses

→ 4. Reveals What We Have in Common (Even If We Look Different)

→ 5. Encourages Dialogue and Greater Understanding

→ 6. Progressive Managers Can Now Address Concerns That Organizations Are Seeking to Learn about Their Workers

1. Personality.
2. Interests.
3. Skills.
4. Aspirations.
5. Experiences.
6. Education.

—Twenty-five questions that get to the individual or the "soul" of people.

1. Work ethic.
2. Ambition/ Energy level.
3. Knowledge.
4. Creativity.
5. Motivation.
6. Sincerity.
7. Outlook.
8. Collegiality/Collaborativeness.
9. Curiosity.
10. Judgment/ Maturity.
11. Integrity.

and New Mexico and me in the Northeast), and although both of us like watching basketball on TV, we are both pretty uncoordinated on the court. "I see what you mean, boss. I can think of at least six or seven questions that I could be asking people about their interests."

"And you'll find," added the CEO, "that even though you and that other person might look very different on the surface, you may have a lot in common. But you only realize that if you start off with a focus on these Proversity Characteristics."

"I see what you mean. So for skills, I might find out if he speaks a foreign language, or has some nonbusiness related skill that I also might share."

"Exactly, Percy. Maybe you both are great at operating or designing computer programs. And moving on to the next Proversity characteristic, you'd learn more about his aspirations once you ask about his short-term and long-term goals. And those might happen to overlap with yours as well. He also might have had similar and interesting childhood school experiences, overlapping work experiences, sibling rivalry experiences—maybe even had the same size family or also had a grandparent live with him, like you did." The CEO smiled and pointed to boxes 3, 4, and 5. "Do you see how your questions can elicit unique responses that force you to see the real person—the *soul* of the person—as opposed to a stereotype that has no relation to reality?"

"Yes I do see, chief. And I also see how these individual answers might reveal that we have something in common even if we appear very different on the surface."

The CEO nodded while looking over at the NFC eagle on his desk. "And Percy, when you start to reach this level of dialogue—a dialogue that gets beyond face value, to where you really learn about a person, you can reach that very important sixth box on the Proversity Paradigm. This is the last and most important step. Here, you get to address the crucial concerns that Progressive Managers need to address when they are examining the workers that are joining their organizations and teams."

12

The Proversity Awareness Game™

Marsha stood in the center of the room as Percy and the other committee members created a circle with ten chairs. Each chair was turned outward. It was the third meeting of the 100th Anniversary Committee.

"Now, tell me Marsha," Chris asked with exasperation in his voice. "What's the point of this little exercise when we've already got too much to do on this committee?"

"Excellent question," added Sylvia. "I have enough phone messages on my desk to keep me in the office all weekend. I honestly could find better use for this time."

Percy knew that the committee members had lost a lot of their interest in working with him on this project. And it was obvious to him that when he failed to connect with them, he also failed to get them inspired about each other and their mandate. He'd done such a bad job at the first meeting, he knew he may only have one more opportunity to pull the group together. He hoped that the CEO's game would help.

"The exercise we are about to start is called *The Proversity Awareness Game,*™" explained Marsha, "and the boss says we should all try it before we move on with our committee work."

Austin rolled his eyes and shook his head at Calvin. Masako crossed her arms and shook her head at Percy. No one was thrilled about being there.

Percy surveyed the circle of chairs while Marsha climbed into the circle and taped a number on the back of each chair so that it could be seen by the person in the middle of the circle.

"The CEO says that whenever a group of unfamiliar people like us come together," Percy began, as he thought about the CEO's lesson on the best way to find good workers, "they should spend time trying to discover the Proversity that exists among them. So even if we look different, there may be many things that we share. He says it will first, help us get along better, and then next, help us work more productively."

"How much more do we *need* to know about each other?" Austin asked as Marsha assigned him to chair number three. "This is like those corny games my social studies teacher made us play in junior high. I think we already get along well enough."

"I can agree with that," Masako added sarcastically as she was given her assigned chair.

Once all of the coworkers were given their seat numbers, they sat down in the circle of chairs.

Percy and Marsha had agreed that Marsha would serve as moderator for the game. Although he was skeptical of it, they both agreed that he stood to gain more from being a participant in one of the chairs than the moderator who would be standing in the middle.

As Marsha moved into the middle of the circle, with everyone's back to her, she explained how the Proversity Awareness Game worked. "The purpose of this game is for us to learn how much we have in common with people that we originally thought were completely different from us. Normally, we look at people, size them up and decide if they *look* like people that we should pay attention to. We too often ignore them if they look different from us."

"I hate to be a downer, Marsha," added Phillip. "But you and Percy don't really think this is going to make our work on this Committee go any faster, do you?"

"Look," Percy said, "we're not trying to work a miracle here. We just want to try out something that may give us an additional way to communicate. Frankly, this game is most beneficial in groups where no one has met before. Think of it as a potential exercise that we might recommend to our human resources department when they bring in new recruits who have never met. If it helps our group just a little, think about what it may do for new hires who have never met before or worked together."

"We see people, and decide if they look like people that we should listen to."

Marsha nodded and gestured to the group. "People, that's the attitude we need here: an open mind. Maybe it'll do only a little for us, but the Proversity Awareness Game may be the ideal exercise for coworkers who are just getting to know one another for the first time."

Percy listened intently and thought about the messy situation that had developed with Ann and with Austin. He could see his promotion disappearing in front of his eyes. He knew he owed it to the CEO, himself, and to the 100th Anniversary team to make their year-long project work. He was willing to try anything to prove to himself that he could be the kind of Progressive Manager that the CEO and others would respect.

"There's one thing that doesn't make sense to me," Austin said while sitting in his chair. "We can't really see each other sitting this way. Isn't it easier to learn about people by talking to each other face-to-face?"

Marsha walked around the inside of the circle with an inch-high stack of special index cards. "Good question, Number 3. And by the way, I'll be calling on people by number and not by name. But to answer your question, Number 3, the reason why we don't have you address each other face-to-face is because too many interactions are governed by the physical characteristics that we see in front of us. Too often we focus only on a person's complexion, clothing, gestures, physical handicap, hair, or other obvious feature that distracts us from the verbal message that they are trying to convey. It may sound like an old stereotype, but many women complain that when they talk to some men—even in business settings—the guy will be focusing more on the woman's legs or chest than on what she is saying."

"I'm Number 7 and I know how that feels, but from a different perspective," added Mark. "On days when I need to bring my walker to work or when it's sitting in my office, I feel like I better hide it because people stare at it when I'm trying to talk to them. Before I had developed multiple sclerosis, I always felt I had people's full attention when I spoke."

Percy interrupted. "And Marsha, to add to Number 7's point, the CEO says that we are more likely to listen to the content of what a person says if we aren't reminding ourselves that the speaker looks different from our expectations. If we keep noting that they look different, we tell ourselves that we can't possibly have anything in common to discuss. We aren't getting past face value that way. We get stuck on diversity—the differences—and we don't move forward."

Marsha nodded. "Good point, Number 6. I'm sure you've all been in a situation where you were looking at someone while they spoke to you at a social event and you didn't hear a word they were saying because you were simultaneously telling yourself, 'Why is this person talking to me? Just look at him, we obviously have nothing in common. He's so much older, or gay, or Korean, or dark skinned, or conservative, etc.' Well, committee members, that's what we want to get beyond here. We're trying to get past face value. Even though you may very well recognize each other's voices as we play this game, you will pay more attention to finding out if the other person says something that relates to you, your work, or your life."

"So what are the rules of this Proversity Awareness Game?" Dan asked. "I assume we're not allowed to turn around, to our sides, or look into the center of the circle. Right?"

"That's right, Number 4," Marsha answered. "Each of you knows your own seat number, and you should indicate your desire to speak by raising your hand. Everything said in this room is to remain confidential. I want people to talk about themselves based upon the questions I ask or the comments I make. All of my questions or comments are going to come from this special stack of index cards that have been written out in advance. Each card has a different question printed on it. When the first person responds to my comment, and starts talking, and he or she hits upon something that you have in common, quickly write it down on your pad in two or three words, then raise your hand so that I can call on you to speak. At each interchange, you can talk for up to 30 seconds."

Karl raised his hand.

"Yes, Number 1."

"I'm getting a little confused by these rules, so why don't we just start and you correct us as we go?"

Percy agreed even though he was still skeptical that he would discover that he had much in common with anyone in the room. "Good idea. We don't have to get this perfect. We just have to see if it helps improve our communications and whether it might help others. So Marsha, if it's okay with everyone else, you should start when you're ready."

Everybody nodded.

Marsha looked at her first index card. "Okay, now remember to raise your hand when you hear something that you have in common with what you hear. And it's up to you, but before you raise your hand, you may want to jot a quick word or two down just in case I don't get to you on the first call and you end up forgetting your point. Some of the cards have questions and some just make statements. Here we go. The first card asks, 'How will you spend your free time once you leave work at the end of the week?' I'll start us off. This weekend I am going to an orchard to go apple picking with my sister and her two kids. On Saturday night I will probably rent a couple of suspense movies and—"

Before Marsha finished her remarks, two hands went up.

She looked at seat Number 2, Phillip.

"I hope I'm not cutting in too fast, but this weekend my church is sponsoring apple-picking trips for kids that live in the city." Phillip paused and nodded as he continued. "During the summer, we take them on camping trips to Camp Siwanoy."

Then a hand went up from seat Number 5, Calvin. Marsha turned. "Okay Number 5, you have something in common with that. Tell us what you want to add."

Calvin felt a little awkward, but went ahead, "Next weekend, I am going with my son's Boy Scout troop to a camporee near Camp Siwanoy—about two hours from here. My son is a hard-core city kid and hates camping out, so we made a bargain two years ago that if I became assistant scoutmaster, he would agree to join the group. I think it's good for kids to join activities like this and I know he'll eventually like it even though his school friends aren't Boy Scouts, but you wouldn't believe the things I have to do to get my kids to join or try new activities. No matter what I suggest, they hate it."

Another hand went up. "Talk about getting kids to do things they hate," Masako added. "My Dad pushed me into taking racquetball lessons on the weekends just because my older brother wanted to play it. I felt like such an oddball. What kind of 10-year-old suburban Maryland girl plays racquetball? All my other girlfriends were playing volleyball and tennis. I hated the first couple of years because I felt like a tomboy, but I continued it through college just for the exercise. I still play every now and then to get a workout."

Percy couldn't believe his ears. He wanted to raise his hand, but he was totally stunned. He recognized Calvin's voice and never imagined that Calvin would have had anything to do with the Boy Scouts, a group that Percy thought of as more American and more middle class and suburban than anything. He was a scoutmaster at his own son's troop. *Why didn't this ever come up in my conversations with Calvin before? Masako on a racquetball court? I always wanted to know how to play, but I never would have thought that she would be into sports of any kind.*

Another hand. Mark laughed, "I know this is off the topic, but you grew up in Maryland? What town? I grew up in Washington, DC, and worked on the docks in Annapolis for two summers."

Marsha shuffled her stack of index cards, then pulled out another as she stood in the circle with everyone's back to her. "Okay, here's a good one on another topic: It says, 'Sometimes I'm sorry that I started my career so far away from the hometown where my parents live. Sometimes I think it would be nice to drop in and get a home-cooked meal, or to know that they can look in and take care of my cats and plants when I go away. Holiday visits and phone calls are never enough.' "

Karl's hand went up.

"Number 1?"

"I feel the same way—especially since my parents live in another country and I only get to see them every two years." Karl paused. "And I worry about their health, but because of the distance, I can't keep up with their doctors or their diets. Even the phone calls get to be too expensive."

Dan's hand went up. "I used to feel the same way, but it's no piece of cake having a parent living under your nose either. My wife and I moved my Dad into our guest room last year when my Mom died and we started noticing my Dad was forgetting things and locking himself out of the house. Now, he worries me to death because there's some new problem every week. I don't know if he's trying to get more of our attention, or if he's really this absent-minded now that my Mom is gone."

Sylvia nodded as Dan finished his remarks and Marsha turned to her. "Number 8?"

"I hate to be a downer," added Sylvia, "but you should see if your father is showing early signs of Alzheimer's disease. My uncle started calling me last year to say that his housekeeper and his neighbor were stealing his mail and his daily newspapers. We thought he was just being dramatic because he was bored, but we learned that he was actually in the early stages of Alzheimer's. He had actually forgotten that he'd already read or thrown out the new mail."

Then Marsha pulled out another index card from her deck. "Here's one that's more work-related: It says, 'The one thing that surprised me the most about working in a large corporation was . . . .' "

During the next half hour, as Percy sat in seat Number 6 listening to the comments of his fellow committee members, he realized he wasn't alone. He was stunned by what he could learn about others—and himself—if he just closed his eyes and listened to what they were saying. It was not something that he had been used to doing.

13

A Progressive Manager's 12 Commandments

"Percy," asked the CEO, "how did the Proversity Awareness Game work for you and Marsha at your last 100th Anniversary Committee meeting?"

"It was quite enlightening! It seemed a little hokey in the beginning, but it amazed me when I realized how little I had known about people on the Committee, and it was surprising to discover how much closer you listen to people when you're not looking at them and judging them by their physical characteristics." Percy paused. "Of course, I knew who was talking from recognizing their voices, but I kept more of a focus on what they said—just to see what I had in common with them."

The CEO nodded. "Well, just imagine how it would work for new groups of workers who are meeting each other for the first time. That's who it is really intended for."

Percy had only raised his hand a couple times in the session, but that was only because he was so taken by how much he'd never listened to before.

"So you think it was beneficial, Percy?"

Beneficial for everyone except Austin, who mocked the idea and laughed at me for going along with it. Austin never gives an inch, and it was obvious to everybody in the room.

"It was definitely beneficial."

"Great," said the CEO. "Now that you've okayed the Proversity Awareness Game, I think we can make that a formal part of our orientation when we bring in new employees or form new task forces at NFC."

"Wow. I'm glad I could help," said Percy, feeling pleased.

"That's good to hear," offered the CEO, "because I'd like for you to move to the next level and start coming up with other ideas that can help create better communication around here. Why don't you start with the cafeteria situation?"

"The cafeteria?"

"Yes, Percy. I think you know what I mean. I don't like what goes on in our cafeteria. And although it's not very different than what goes on in most other corporate lunchrooms—or elementary or high school lunchrooms, for that matter—I don't like how it polarizes people." The CEO paused. "So why don't you try to come up with a solution for that? Okay?"

Percy had no idea of where he'd come up with a solution for this problem. *I'm not a psychologist. How can I get people to change habits that they've lived with for so long?*

"Not that I'm complaining, Sir, but why should *I* be the one to solve this problem? This seems like an issue that the human resources department should be addressing." Percy paused, "I'm a line manager, Sir. This is really outside my jurisdiction, if you know what I mean."

"I hear what you're saying, Percy," replied the CEO. "But encouraging appropriate behavior among our employees should not be left just to the human resources department. It is everybody's responsibility to encourage open-mindedness, and I think the message should start at the top, with the senior executives. Don't lose sight of the fact that line managers have a responsibility to get people to communicate appropriately in the workplace."

"He wants you to do *what?*" Ann was just as surprised as Percy.

"Fix the problem with the cafeteria." Percy studied a small drawing that showed the layout of tables in the company cafeteria. "If this is his way of holding back my promotion, I'll tell you Ann, it just may work because this is a real tough problem to solve. You know, over at White Light, they even have separate lunchrooms."

Ann leaned against her computer keyboard. "Well, I must admit. You would please a whole lot of company office managers and high school principals around the country if you could come up with a way to change our cafeteria and share the idea with other cafeterias that are filled with segregated tables. Maybe there's a way to solve the problem. I wouldn't give up yet."

"Sir," explained Percy when he went back upstairs three hours later. "It's not that I'm saying I can't solve the problem. I just need some kind of guidelines on this." Percy was back in the CEO's office asking for help on dealing with the cafeteria situation. He had brought the issue up in his lunchtime meeting with the Anniversary Committee hoping they'd have some ideas. Now he needed even more suggestions. "I don't want to give the committee some moral lecture," Percy added, "but to get their support, I feel like I've got to lay some groundwork or set some moral standards for ourselves. Does that make any sense?"

The CEO opened up his desk drawer, and as usual, was able to find some papers that could address the situation. He handed Percy a sheet of paper. "That makes a lot of sense, and this may help you out. I call them my 12 Commandments—a Progressive Manager's 12 Commandments—and they

A Progressive Manager's 12 Commandments

1. I will show equal respect to coworkers regardless of their position or tenure in my organization.

2. I will work to create an environment where my coworkers and customers have permission to both discuss our differences and look for characteristics and ideas that we all share.

3. I will not judge my coworkers on the basis of their gender, race, ethnicity, national origin, religion, sexual orientation, age, or handicap status.

4. I will stand up to those coworkers who seek to divide or discriminate against customers, clients, and others in my organization.

5. I will recognize that certain decisions I make outside my organization may have an impact on individuals inside my organization.

6. I will reach out to mentor others in my organization who feel excluded.

7. I will try to build bridges between my organization and the outside community.

8. I will accept criticism and constructive suggestions without taking offense.

9. I will acknowledge others when they make contributions and I will recognize that any gain they receive is also a gain for our organization.

(Continued)

A Progressive Manager's
12 Commandments
(Continued)

10. I will help myself and others by addressing our own passive bias and by encouraging them to get past "face value."
11. I will maintain an open-minded progressive approach to building my organization.
12. I will become a progressive manager because I am a leader who values Proversity and change—even when others are pushing the status quo.

---

will help you advance Proversity throughout this organization. They'll help you lay the perfect moral foundation for the committee's work," explained the CEO. "I think you have a firm grasp on how Proversity works, so I think that it's time for you to consider some standard rules to run an office by. Maybe these will help guide you on the cafeteria situation."

14

Meeting Others Halfway

"This stuff is nuts!" said Austin as he looked at the rubber-backed computer mousepad in his hand. "He actually spent money on this?"

The other committee members were reading the Progressive Manager's 12 Commandments that were printed out on their computer mousepads. When Ann finished passing them out around the table, she turned to Marsha and Percy. "Mr. McGee, will there be anything else?"

"Yeah," Austin answered sarcastically. "You can tattoo the *Star Spangled Banner* across my forehead."

"That'll be enough, Austin," Percy interrupted as he stood up before the committee. "As you can all see, I had the Progressive Manager's 12 Command-ments reproduced by our printing department this weekend and had them printed onto your computer mousepad. I've decided that the greatest impact that this 100th Anniversary Committee can have is to not just celebrate the company's history, but also to help implement some important changes that will shape its future—the first of which was to add the Proversity Awareness Game to NFC's new-hire orientation program."

Marsha nodded. "Furthermore, at Percy's suggestion, we are thinking of making these 12 Commandments a centerpiece on the project. We feel that we should send a strong message to all the employees that we won't tolerate bigotry or narrow-mindedness at NFC."

"And if I might add," Percy continued, "Marsha and I feel that our goals are best accomplished if we give people values and guidelines to direct us in our work. And the commandments will be our values and guidelines. Now I know you're wondering about these computer mousepads, but since people spend so much time at their desktop computers, we figured we should print the 12 Commandments in a place where NFC employees will be reminded of them every day."

"Hence, the mousepads," added Marsha. "What we want to do is make one of these for every employee and vendor/customer that we work with or sell to—and across the bottom of the pad—below the 12 Commandments, would be the phrase "Celebrating 100 Years at National Flashlight Company."

"Okay," asked Dan. "But what comes next? We hand out mousepads and that's it?"

"No," Percy answered. "We next figure out how to incorporate these commandments into our work day and our dealings with others, and one of my ideas is to address the cafeteria situation."

"I assume you mean the separate tables?" Karl asked. "Because I never saw so much segregation until I got to this country."

"Well, it's not that anybody ever forced people to sit at specific tables, Karl," Calvin added. "It's just that people choose to separate themselves. It's a voluntary decision."

"And what difference does it make?" asked Austin. "I sit with my friends. Who cares if we just want to sit with people who make us feel comfortable?"

"Because the logical conclusion drawn from that is that there are many more people who make us feel *uncomfortable*," Marsha answered. "And if we are uncomfortable with *eating* around people who are a little different, then we are surely not going to feel inspired to respect each other in a teamworking situation. One logically follows the other."

Percy nodded, "This is a problem that starts at an early age, and although I've never talked about it with my kids, I've seen how my six-year-old daughter and her classmates separate themselves in her lunch room at school. We adults are afraid to work or socialize with each other because we learned to be afraid as kids. Kids in my daughter's school cafeteria are separating themselves at tables based on race, religion, ethnic group, and gender. They have their minds made up about each other before they've even met each other."

Sylvia agreed. "That's how it was at my school when I was growing up. I sat where I knew I was supposed to sit."

"Me, too," Calvin added.

"Same with me and my two brothers," added Mark.

"I guess we just didn't have permission to get to know anybody who was different," said Sylvia.

"Well," Percy interrupted. "That's what we're going to do at NFC—starting with the cafeteria. We're going to give people the permission to meet people who look different on the surface. Like it says in the second commandment, let's create an environment in the cafeteria that will allow people to accept differences."

Austin raised his hand. "People, don't you think this is getting a little out of hand? Now, it's not that I have anything against anybody in this room or this company, but—"

Percy rolled his eyes, but remained silent. *Why is Austin always getting in the way of every new idea I have?*

"And I'm not one to get in the way of your new ideas, Percy," Austin said, "but let's be honest. Lunch is the only time that people can kick back and relax. The reason why people like to eat with their own kind is because they're talking about things they all agree with and understand. It's not that I don't want to be sitting with Karl and the other foreigners, but—"

"Internationals," Karl interrupted.

"Internationals—excuse me, or the girls like Marsha or—"

"Women!" snapped Marsha.

"Or the crippled—" continued Austin as he pointed at Dan's metal walker.

"We call ourselves *disabled.*"

"Okay, disabled—or the Spanish people," Austin added as he gestured toward Sylvia.

"That's Hispanic or Latino."

"Well, you all know what I mean," Austin insisted. "It's just that we want to be around people who talk the same way and about the same stuff."

Calvin nodded. "In a way, he's right. I don't sit with the women because I don't want to spend the whole lunch hour talking about dieting and shopping."

Sylvia looked up. "And what makes you think we all talk about dieting? You've never sat with us before. We talk about lots of things. Today, in fact, Louise and I were talking about how much we should be putting into the NFC pension plan."

Calvin looked a little surprised.

Percy interrupted. "You see Calvin, you and I don't even know what Sylvia is talking about at lunch. Everybody is making a lot of assumptions about each table based on face value—what it looks like from our perspective."

"That sounds nice and open-minded Percy," added Mark, "but you can't come out and criticize people just for sitting with their own kind."

Percy pushed his point, "But it's not just that people sit with their own kind, it's that no one has the courage to break this imaginary rule."

"Well, from what I see, there's a reason," said Karl. "Nobody wants to get ostracized. I sit with the other international workers even when there are times that I see someone else that I want to sit with. But I stay put because I don't want to get talked about."

Austin nodded. "If I left the table I usually sit at and went and sat at Calvin's table, Calvin and the other black guys would wonder what the hell I thought I was doing, and my white friends would think I turned on them or something."

Calvin looked at Percy and then nodded. "He's sort of right. My folks would think I'd sold out or something if I all of a sudden left the black table and started eating with the white guys."

"So how do we do it?" Phillip finally asked. "How are we going to change this?"

Percy smiled. "Well, I have an idea that might give people the chance to break these imaginary rules. Since most people eat lunch in the cafeteria Monday through Thursday, why not give people randomly assigned seats every other Monday. There are 36 tables in the cafeteria." He put up the drawing of the cafeteria layout on the overhead slide projector. Each table was numbered. "I always sit with the same guys at table number 22 and we've been doing it for more than two years. And I know Calvin sits at table number 16, and Marsha usually is with the same people at table number 4. Next Monday, we could either assign people to a specific table with an eye to intentionally mixing people. Or we could have them pick a number out of a hat when they walk into the cafeteria. That way, people go to whichever table they got by chance."

"This seems so controlled to me," added Phillip. "I agree we should mix more, but lunchtime is usually the only time I get to relax and get to know people."

Percy turned off the projector and looked around the room. "I agree it's a time to get to know people, but we want everyone to get to know other people, new people—*all* people."

Marsha agreed, "It's only once every two weeks—or maybe once every three weeks. It's just a way to give people permission to mix more. Who knows? You might meet somebody on that Monday and like them so much that you choose to seek them out the next day. We might want to measure response by using a simple survey at the end of each week. It's a start. Percy, I think it's a great idea. People may resist it at first, but you've got my support."

15

Big Brother—
Big Sister

Four weeks had passed and Percy called the Committee together again to discuss the success of the Cafeteria Project they had implemented. He and the rest of the Committee had agreed to try the plan on an accelerated basis using four consecutive Mondays as days where employees would be randomly reassigned to table numbers that they drew from a box when they entered the cafeteria.

"I am happy to give you a report on the Cafeteria Project," explained Percy as he addressed the members of the Anniversary Committee.

"As you know, we distributed surveys to employees on the last four Fridays asking people to give us their views of our Cafeteria Monday Mixers."

Marsha nodded at Percy. "And as you also know, before the first Monday Mixer took place, we had Maintenance remove two of the tables from the lunchroom and then had them reconfigure the layout of the lunch room so people would not be inclined to look at the room in terms of where they always *used* to sit."

Karl smiled. "Well I don't think we really fooled anybody with that. People could approximate where their table had been before."

"That's true," Marsha answered, "but we wanted to let people know that this is a fresh start."

"So what were the results?" Marsha asked. "Because I thought the first two Mondays were a little comical. I was assigned to table 7 the first Monday and then table 15 the next Monday. I felt like I was in first grade—being told where to go."

Calvin laughed. "To tell you the truth, I thought it was kind of fun—just to see who I was going to get put with. Of course, I went back to my normal group of friends on both Tuesdays—just so we could talk about who we'd gotten stuck with the day before."

"Calvin, that's exactly what many of our surveys told us," Percy interrupted. "During the first two weeks, most of the people went back to the original group of friends they ate with before we started the project. But interestingly, when we looked at the third week of surveys, things started to change. We looked at the survey question where we asked people 'Have you met anyone at your randomly assigned tables for the first time that you would consider eating with or socializing with in the future?'"

"And that's when we started to learn that during the third week," Marsha explained, "people were adding new faces to their groups. Of course, some tables didn't change much at all—but others became more random."

Sylvia raised her hand. "Well, I'll tell you one thing. During the last couple weeks, I've noticed people stopping off at other lunch tables just to say hello or to talk to people they'd met on the prior Monday—so something is obviously happening."

Austin rolled his eyes and crossed his arms as others nodded at Sylvia.

Phillip also nodded enthusiastically, "I agree that this is turning into something good, but I think we better go to our original plan of having the Monday Mixers every second or third week. We don't want to burn people out with it."

"That's very true," Percy added. "We just tried to do several in a row to see if it would have any effect at moving people closer together. It may be a long process, but I think it's doing what we hoped."

"In the meantime," Marsha remarked "I think it's a good idea for us to review the Progressive Manager's 12 Commandments and see what other areas might be worth examining. Percy, you had talked about using the 12 Commandments as values and guidelines that would help us address other problems at NFC. Does anyone have ideas they want to discuss?"

"An issue I'd like to address as we find other ways to incorporate the 12 Commandments is the idea of mentors," added Sylvia. "I'm looking at the sixth commandment on mentors, and I agree that mentoring is important if we want to encourage new hires and give greater guidance to people who show promise."

Percy thought about the many mentors he'd had since he had first come to NFC. Some had left and gone over to White Light, but a few of them were still here. Although the CEO had told him that some people find it difficult to find mentors, he could think of at least five people who had mentored him in different ways in the last four years. "Yes, Sylvia, I agree. What's your suggestion?"

"Well Percy, I'm a little annoyed and a little embarrassed to admit this, but nobody has ever tried to mentor me, and I think it's because of what I am. I've seen a lot of my colleagues get mentors without even looking for them." Sylvia suddenly stopped speaking and looked around the table.

Austin slammed his palm on the table top. "Oh give me a break, Sylvia. Let's not turn this into a racist and sexist thing here. You can't tell me that people aren't mentoring you because we're all a bunch of bigots."

"That's not what I'm saying, Austin. I'm just saying that no one has ever volunteered to mentor me."

"Me either," added Masako.

Phillip agreed. "I agree with her too. Nobody's ever tried to mentor me, and I'm sure it's because they're all afraid of gay people. Straight people want to mentor straight people."

Austin rolled his eyes and mumbled something to himself.

Percy nodded, "Sylvia and Phillip, I had been thinking of some way in which we might assign mentors to every person who has never had one for the very point you're both making."

Karl wasn't convinced. "But isn't mentoring supposed to be a natural process where a senior employee looks out for and guides somebody else because they happen to like and feel comfortable around the junior employee? It shouldn't have to be forced on someone."

Percy thought about what the CEO had explained to him earlier. "Well Karl, all of you are making good points. Yes, mentoring is supposed to be a natural process where a senior person voluntarily chooses a junior protege. The problem is that the senior people pick people who make them feel comfortable. And who makes them feel comfortable? People who are just like them. Think about who your mentors have been: Hans is from Austria and Paul is from Germany."

Marsha nodded, "These senior bosses mentor employees who remind them of themselves. Hans and Paul may have chosen to mentor you only because you come from the same part of Europe. Mentors sometimes only pick proteges who look like themselves, who went to the same schools, who will fit in at their restricted clubs, laugh at their occasional bigoted jokes, or understand their cultural biases."

"That's right," Percy added. "They handpick people—usually guys who they'd like to hang out with. So even though they aren't consciously telling themselves 'I don't want to mentor that Asian woman, that gay coworker, or that disabled guy,' they are inevitably always picking their own kind in the narrowest sense. So I'd say we should start a policy of assigning mentors to those employees who feel left out."

"It may be a good idea to create some guidelines or instructions," added Dan, "because some people don't know how to go about mentoring a person."

Percy was energized by the Committee members' enthusiastic input. He was glad they saw the need to work the Commandments into NFC's policies and realized there were probably an endless number of issues that could be addressed.

"And since you mentioned the topic of mentors taking people to restricted clubs," added Calvin, "I'd like us to come up with a policy that prevents NFC from having company parties at private country clubs that discriminate. I see a direct tie between outside clubs that executives join and the fifth commandment on this list."

"I agree," added Percy. "And let's go a step further and insist that although NFC pays for top level executives to belong to clubs, let's create a policy that says NFC will no longer pay for memberships at any club that is not integrated by race, religion, and gender. That includes Greenlawn, too, because I've already written to them to let them know I'm pulling out of there unless they change their rules."

Austin was not the only committee member to be stunned by Percy's remarks.

"You're really starting to impress me," said Masako. "I have to tell you that this is really becoming an enlightening experience for all of us, Percy."

As Percy smiled back at Masako, he thought about the promise that he'd made to Ann. She had endured such an awful time because of his and Austin's behavior.

"Well, I think we also need to establish a person or committee that can receive grievances from people who want to complain about sexual or racial harassment," added Percy as he looked pointedly at Austin. "Because often harassing comments or jokes lead to actual employment discrimination. So let's create a policy that addresses that as well."

By the end of the meeting, the Committee had drawn up eight new proposed goals:

1. Recognizing that some employees are unable to develop relationships with senior colleagues who can advise and guide them, each new hire at NFC shall be assigned to a mentor. And to encourage that mentor to perform his duties, his bonus compensation shall be tied to his success in this area.

2. To eliminate the artificial barriers that have kept the lunchroom from being a more welcoming place, we shall encourage greater mixing among people by choosing one day each month and seating employees by lottery number.

3. To permit a greater flow of information and prevent situations where certain people are unaware of career opportunities at NFC, we shall create a job posting procedure where no position will be interviewed for until it is advertised in a prominent place in the lunch room, human resources office, and in a monthly mailing to all employees.

4. To create an atmosphere where employees feel that they can discuss issues of bias and to create programs that foster greater relations between people of different backgrounds, we will establish a Proversity Committee that is made up of line managers from every department as well as staff managers from each NFC office.

5. As a means to address grievances related to issues of bias, and as a means to resolve disputes between employees on such issues within the company, we shall appoint a Proversity Ombudsman who will receive grievances and attempt to serve as moderator between the parties.

6. In order to address the inability for certain individuals to tap into career-building networks, we shall encourage employees to form company-sanctioned networking groups that discuss issues such as time management, job development skills, and career planning strategies.

7. Recognizing that there are some institutions that continue to discriminate against others on the basis of race, gender, ethnicity, age, sexual orientation, religion, handicap status, color, and national origin, we insist that the company no longer hold events or pay for memberships at any private club that supports such divisive policies.

8. Acknowledging that combating the issue of bias is an ongoing struggle, we direct NFC to invite outside speakers and presenters to discuss such issues and encourage open-mindedness and sensitivity at least three times each year for employees at all levels.

Percy was inspired by the energy and enthusiasm of the committee members. Each of them seemed eager to find more ways to implement the CEO's Commandments and to further enlighten the NFC workforce.

With the 100th Anniversary Committee's approval, Percy and Marsha agreed to submit the eight proposals to the CEO and to continue to solicit other ideas from NFC employees.

16

A Universe of Contacts

"As you know, Percy," explained the CEO as he stood near the large picture window in his office, "I was very impressed to see the eight goals that you and the Anniversary Committee submitted to me. I believe they are all policies worthy of implementing at NFC."

Percy smiled. "Well thank you, Sir, I'm glad you feel that way."

"In fact," the CEO added, "I was so impressed by how they adopted our Proversity mindset, I sent a copy of the goals over to our friends at White Light. Hopefully they will consider using them as well. As you know, they could use some help in this area."

"Well I doubt that White Light will ever be able to accomplish as much as we have in this area," Percy added with a smug grin. "We are already—"

"Before you go any further," interrupted the CEO. "Let's not get full of ourselves, Percy. It's our duty to share our ideas with others on the outside too. You've done a good job so far, but things still aren't where I want them to be. You have to realize that an employee will never be a successful Progressive Manager until he learns how to deal with those around him—and I don't just mean those that report to him."

"Sure," Percy agreed. "That makes sense, but I'm already dealing with everyone around me. I've got my staff in line, and I've improved my interactions with our salespeople and many of my colleagues in other departments as well." Percy thought of his meeting yesterday with Ann where they discussed the issue of sexual harassment and what further policies or programs will be created to educate people on the problem.

"That's true, Percy. You've done an excellent job with your colleagues, customers, and direct reports, but I think you're forgetting some other people that are in your universe."

Percy thought for a moment. "My universe? I don't think I know what people you mean."

The CEO went over to his flipchart and showed Percy an illustration that had a series of circles on it. There was one big circle in the middle with the letters "P.M." Around that circle, were 12 other smaller circles—making the picture look like a solar system—12 planets revolving around a sun. Twelve arrows radiated from the sun, each one pointing to a different planet.

"This is the Progressive Manager's Universe of Contacts," said the CEO.

"The *what?*"

"Percy, these are all the people you must include in your universe. If you truly want to be a Progressive Manager and one day run this or any other organization, you will have to learn to deal with all the different entities operating in the Progressive Manager's Universe."

Percy looked at the page. Each of the "planets" or entities had a different label in it. Moving clockwise around the "universe" beginning at one o'clock, there was Special Interest Groups, the Community, Media, Recruitment Resources, Underrepresented Groups in the Organization, Governmental Bodies and Regulators, Consumers, All Co-workers and Employees, Vendors, Senior Bosses, Board Members and Shareholders, and Close Personal Relationships.

"Wow!" Percy was mesmerized. "You don't mean to say that I've got to keep up with all those different groups and entities?"

The CEO shook his head. "Why do you think I've got this diagram hanging in my office? I even have it on the back of my desk calendar. Of course, you can't interact with each of these groups every-day—and some may not even relate to the job you currently hold, but you must remind yourself of these people as often as possible. You must know that you are responding to them, building a relationship with them, serving them—and most of all, treating them with respect. Your job demands that you respect and interact with more than just those who directly report to you."

"For example," said the CEO as he pointed to a couple of the circles on the chart, "you have

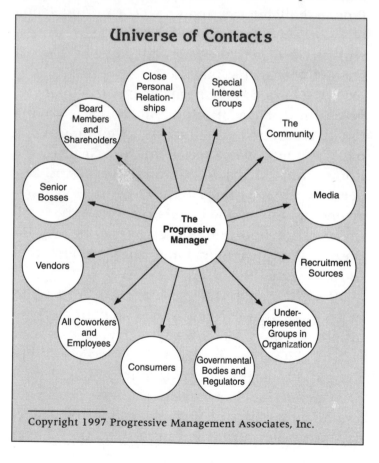

Universe of Contacts

- Close Personal Relationships
- Special Interest Groups
- Board Members and Shareholders
- The Community
- Senior Bosses
- Media
- Vendors
- Recruitment Sources
- **The Progressive Manager**
- All Coworkers and Employees
- Underrepresented Groups in Organization
- Consumers
- Governmental Bodies and Regulators

Copyright 1997 Progressive Management Associates, Inc.

learned to be sensitive to the diverse concerns of your coworkers and your vendors."

Percy looked at the "Consumers" entity. "I think I've also reached out to a diverse group of consumers, too. After that first meeting with the White Light people, I immediately asked the promotions people to make sure our sales force was offering multilingual sales brochures and last week Marsha and I directed all salespeople to give customers evaluation forms so they could send in and comment on how they were being treated."

The CEO nodded and looked at the entities on the right side of the diagram. "And what about over here?" he asked.

Percy looked at the Community, Media, and Recruitment Sources contacts on the chart.

"Are you reaching out to a broad range of community groups, media people, and recruitment sources, Percy?"

"Well, we've talked about donating some lighting products to several of the local nursing homes and we are advertising on a couple of black radio stations."

The CEO shook his head. "No, Percy. I mean *real* contact. I want to see you meeting some of the heads of local community groups. You should be meeting the heads of minority and women's organizations, religious groups, and others. I want you to meet and know about the people who run the media outlets. And not just the mainstream media—you should know about the black media, the women's press, the gay and lesbian publications, the Chinese radio station, the two Hispanic newspapers, religious media, and so on."

Percy jotted down the CEO's points.

"And you should also be expanding the range of recruiting sources you use to find our salespeople. Let these sources know about our Proversity mindset so they know we want a varied group of employees working at NFC," said the CEO. "Try to recruit from some of the historically black colleges, the religious schools, find out how we can participate in job fairs that are sponsored by women's groups or minority organizations. I heard the Urban League sponsors local and national job fairs. Call the black MBA and the Hispanic MBA organizations and see if they can refer members who are looking for work. Let's advertise in those newsletters that are published by the Asian American Legal Defense Fund, the Families and Work Institute, the UJA, the Lambda Legal Defense Fund, Baptist Convention, American Association of Retired Persons, Catalyst, the NAACP, the National Association of Working Women, and ABLE-DATA since they keep a database for disabled workers. Also see which media or organizations can reach Native Americans since we have done very little to reach those workers."

Percy was amazed that the CEO knew about all of these outside activities. He looked at some of the other contacts: Senior Bosses and Board Members. "And what about those entities on the other side of the diagram? Should I be doing something with them too?"

"If you can, but not all managers would have access to these groups," explained the CEO. "But they are nevertheless relevant to our work and someone in the organization has to communicate our Proversity mindset to them. For example, I have made sure to tell all the senior level executives that their twice-a-year evaluations will include a component which evaluates how well they have done in hiring and retaining a diverse staff. I've also sent a letter to NFC's board members suggesting that they consider making a special effort to expand the board so that we see women, people of color, the disabled, and other less-represented people alongside the white men who have always made up the nine-person board."

Percy was astonished by how far the CEO was willing to take his point. "That's pretty aggressive for you, Sir, to say something like that to the board—the very people that can fire you."

The CEO nodded as he looked at the Universe of Entities. "Perhaps it is, Percy, and I was a little nervous about discussing this at first, but when the board put me in this job, they hired a Progressive Manager. And even if my policies on Proversity make people a little uneasy at first, I know that it's best for the whole company in the end. NFC can only benefit by having more Progressive Managers who have the courage to reach out and make their point to *everyone*."

Percy looked at the entity at the top left: Close Personal Relationships. "And I guess," Percy began "when you say everyone, you mean friends, too?"

"That's right," said the CEO as he looked for a sheet on his desk. "And speaking of friends, let me give you this. It came over the wire services this morning. It's an update on our old friends at White Light, and unfortunately, it's not good news."

Since early last month there had been rumors that the ten-year-old lighting company, White Light Manufacturing Company, had been facing serious business and legal problems. This morning, it was confirmed that the $275 million company was filing for bankruptcy. Industry analysts and others had expressed surprise by White Light's refusal to drop its ineffective White Light Lady sales program which was considered by many in the industry to be an outdated and sexist approach to selling the fast-growing company's light bulbs. The company had also publicly refused to sell their residential products in neighborhoods that they openly referred to as "undesirable communities where people didn't bother to learn English." This afternoon, in Federal Court, it was reported that two major suits will be filed against the company: one a sex discrimination suit and the other a racial discrimination suit—both filed by job applicants who had been refused employment at the company that was notorious for its all-white, all-male management teams.

As Percy stood up with an expression of shock, the CEO stared at him. "I was sorry to hear about this. But you know, this really didn't have to happen to them. White Light refused to move beyond their Passive Bias and look for the Proversity around them. There were people around them that they refused to acknowledge. There were plenty of warning signs."

Percy shook his head. "You're right."

"And Percy, if I were you I would look at that chart closely. Because I think there is someone in your own universe that's standing between you and your becoming a Progressive Manager."

Percy had a good idea of who the CEO was talking about.

17

The Enlightenment

When Percy returned to his desk, he thought about all he had learned over the last few months from the CEO, Ann, and the members of his 100th Anniversary Committee. He felt quite good about the progress they had all made. Over the last few weeks, he had gained the confidence of the team, had established the new cafeteria policy, and had presented the CEO with several proposals that would address bias problems and implement more Proversity at NFC.

As he thumbed through the new company directory that contained the Company's new slogan, "National Flashlight Company—Lighting Our World Every Day," he thought about Austin Butler. Butler was the only uncomfortable spot for Percy. As a close personal relation, he was the only open issue on the CEO's Universe of Contacts. Austin was the only one that refused to contribute to the Committee in a productive manner. The offensive remarks and jokes that he whispered to Percy had worn thin long ago, and it was obvious that Austin wasn't willing to embrace others who he perceived as different.

Percy looked down at the index card taped to his desk. Although he had already memorized them, he once again read the steps for becoming a Progressive Manager. He had dealt with his own passive bias; he had discovered how his focus on Proversity brought him closer to people who, at first, seemed different; he had already started using the 12 Commandments. That was three out of the four steps.

While he understood the need to expand his Universe of Contacts, he had not pushed them as far as he needed. And where he fell short was in pushing Austin—a contact that was closer to him than almost anyone else. This was the part of the Universe that the CEO had warned would be the most difficult to change.

As Percy looked down at Step 4, he knew he had to do something fast. The night before, he had told Ann that now, more than ever, he was finding Austin distracting and disruptive on the Anniversary Committee, and even though Austin had made promises to start treating everyone with respect, people could see through his act. And they often asked Percy how he could remain friends with such a person.

Four Steps to Becoming a Progressive Manager

STEP 1 Recognize—and eliminate—your Passive Bias.

STEP 2 Discover—and use—the power of Proversity.

STEP 3 Apply the Progressive Manager's 12 Commandments.

STEP 4 Expand your Universe of Organizational Contacts.

"Mr. McGee, I appreciate your getting him to apologize and promising to be more respectful to me, and I'm glad you are requiring him to spend those twenty hours in sensitivity training, but I think it's still too little, too late. To be honest, the two of you really pushed me to my limits. Why do you keep hanging around him?" Ann spoke without her usual reticence as she helped Percy look over the blueprints for the new designs that he had proposed for the company statue.

Percy shrugged, "I guess because we've been friends for so long. He is one of my oldest friends at NFC. We went through a lot together at this place. But now I see that I've outgrown him by a long shot. And he's also a liability."

"Well I know that firsthand from the sexist and offensive things he said to me," Ann added. "People at NFC aren't stupid. Mr. McGee, I know I shouldn't be saying this, but if people like me think he's a bigot, then everyone must, too. And if they think that about him, they'll think the same about you."

Percy agreed. "I appreciate your insight, Ann. And that's why I've put a harsh letter in his file and required him to attend the sensitivity training. He's just too divisive. And getting him to apologize or disguise his views is not the solution."

"Well," Ann said. "I hate to say this again, but I'm giving it until the end of the month, and if I get the feeling he's not changing, I'm going to insist on my transfer. I like working with you, Mr. McGee, but I don't want to endure him every time he stops by to visit you."

Percy looked up and saw that a new company directory had been delivered to his "IN" box on his desk. He shifted uncomfortably because he knew it was a matter of minutes before Austin Butler would be arriving.

"Hey, McGee—what's doing?"

Percy looked up and saw Austin enter the office and close the door behind him. "I knew you'd be calling me once these new directories came out." He laughed, "Came down as soon as I got your message. Up for a marathon of NTO? On my way up, I passed a bunch of you-know-what's who were going home for their little holiday tomorrow."

"We've got a problem, Austin."

"Tell me about it, McGee. I was looking through this directory, and us RKO people have shrunk to less than 50 percent of the headquarters office."

Percy leaned toward his friend, "No, Butler, that's not what I mean. And I'm really sick of the way you talk about people here. It really disgusts me."

Austin rolled his eyes. "Oh, come on, McGee. The door is closed. You don't have to get into your Proversity—nonbiased lecture with *me*. Nobody else is around."

Percy looked down at his desk and shook his head.

"Wait until the guys over at White Light get a load of this directory!" Austin scoffed. "They'll never let us live it down. It makes us look like some kind of United Nations—all of these weird DKO people. I really envy Roger and Jim over at White Light. They know what they're doing."

Percy couldn't believe his ears.

"I'd trade places with them in a heart beat."

Percy was incredulous. *I can't believe Austin. He obviously doesn't even read the papers. He sits here and talks about White Light as if it's some great place, and there they are filing for bankruptcy and facing two discrimination suits. For months, they've been ignoring NFC's advice and their own business research on the need to adapt their approach to the changing consumers and changing workplace. They were stubborn and narrow-minded. Just like Austin.*

"White Light has the guts to keep out all these DKO people," continued Austin. "They know the importance of moderation—how to keep those people in their place and hold the line. That's what NFC should have done, instead of making all these changes and letting all these freaks and pseudo-Americans in here."

"You really don't get this, do you, Butler?" Percy was incredulous that his friend was so resistant. If he had managed to alter some of his own thinking about people, why couldn't Austin do the same? Why couldn't Austin budge even a little? "You think that all I've talked about is a joke?"

Austin opened up the directory and took the top off his yellow highlighter marker. "Okay, let's start with the As," he said with a grin. "Let's see how many RKO people are on this page. I'll bet we'll be lucky to find even five of us."

Percy stood up from the desk, "Austin, we've been friends a long time, but I have to ask you something."

Austin continued scanning the page until he came across a name worthy of highlighting. "Now there's one—Casey Adams," he said with a satisfied smile. "Now let's see if—"

"I have to ask you something—and it's important."

"What?" Austin asked.

"Do you think that you have biased views about people because they appear different?"

Austin laughed. "Come on, McGee."

"I'm serious."

"Yeah—okay. I'll admit I don't like a lot of these minorities, women, and gays around here. So what?" Austin was unapologetic.

"And do you want to change your attitude?" Percy asked.

Austin stared back at his friend. "Why should I? I was here first."

That was all Percy needed to hear, "I'm sorry to do this because I know we're friends, but I'm going to have to put you on probation and move you out of sales and into the accounting department for the foreseeable future."

"What?"

"I'm sorry, Austin—I really am. I don't want you with any of our customers."

Austin suddenly stood up. The message was only starting to sink in. "What do you mean taking my clients and putting me into the accounting department?" His eyes seemed to glaze over. "What are you talking about Percy?"

"I'm putting you on probation until you have satisfactorily completed your sensitivity training," Percy answered just above a whisper.

"Are you crazy?" Austin cried. "I told you I apologized to that secretary of yours. I was only messing with her head."

"Austin, that's not the half of it."

"You must be out of your mind, Percy. You can't stick me in some back office doing paper work. I'm a salesman and I should be out with customers."

Percy shook his head slowly. "I wish I could let you do that Austin, but I can't trust you. I just don't think you're learning from all that we've been trying to teach people about Proversity and passive bias."

Percy clutched his armchair tightly and nodded at his friend.

Austin was stunned. He replaced the cap on the tip of the yellow highlighter.

"I'm going to be giving your accounts to somebody else as of this Friday."

"This Friday? Who? Somebody new?"

"Yes." Percy had no idea who he'd hire for the job, but he knew this wasn't going to work.

Austin clenched his fists in disappointment. "Tell me the truth, Percy. Are you moving me because of one of those new quota hires? Is that what you're saying? That you have to bring in a DKO person to fill some government quota?"

It occurred to Percy that Austin really hadn't been listening to what Percy had just explained. And for a brief moment, Percy was tempted to cave in and say something that would save Austin's dignity and possibly preserve their friendship. *I could lie and tell him that a government quota is forcing me to give his job to an affirmative action hire—to a woman, a disabled person, a minority person.*

But Percy resisted. He had to make his point again. He had to tell the truth. He closed his eyes and the words came out. "No, Austin. I'm moving you because I am really seeing what a bigoted person you are and what a bad influence you have on people in this organization. I think we have to help you improve your attitude about other kinds of people and only then can we consider moving you back to your present job. And if there's no improvement, you'll be out of a job altogether."

Before Percy could continue his point, Austin Butler had gotten up from the chair and walked toward the door.

"McGee, you're crazy. I think you've forgotten whose side you're on. There's nothing wrong with my attitude. I'm not changing myself for these people. Who needs this job? I can go over and get a job at White Light. Who needs you?"

As Percy saw his door slam shut, he felt a mixture of disappointment and relief. Confronting Austin was a difficult decision for him to have made, but he knew it had been the right thing.

He also had the feeling that he'd made the final step toward becoming a Progressive Manager. It was a step that was long overdue.

ACKNOWLEDGMENTS

When formulating the core ideas, paradigms, and themes behind the story of *Proversity*, I had a tremendous amount of support from colleagues and friends that went beyond those that work with me at Progressive Management Associates, Inc.

These supporters include Andrea J. Heyward, Betty Walker, Martha Fields and her colleagues at Fields Associates, Rosabeth Moss Kanter, Barry Stein, James Grasfield, Loida N. Lewis, Gail Busby, Steve Emanuel, Elliot Hoffman, Andrew Siegel, Merna Popper, Jim Benerofe, Margaret Morton, Ed Bristow of Fordham University, and of course, Betsy Hart, who challenges me as we analyze new issues from our different viewpoints.

I owe a great deal to those colleagues who sent clippings, stories, statistics, and encouragement: Lawrence Hamdan, Jordan Horvath, Dauna Williams, Marguerite Gritenas, Brad Roth, Elisabeth Radow,

Bruce Wilson, Nancy Linnerooth, Vincent and Barbara Thomas, Alison Leigh Cowan, Mitch Semel, Jeanine Pirro, Keith Heyward, Charles Gropper, Lawrence and Laura Gordon, Teresa Clarke, Anita Jackson, Sheri Betts, Marian and Albert Thomas, Leslie Fagenson, Andre and Allyson Owens, my friends at American Program Bureau, CNN, as well as Bill Maher and Scott Carter who have helped me see the folly in too much "political correctness."

While developing the themes for this book, I had the fortune to draw upon my prior and ongoing experiences with many organizations. Among them, I would most like to thank individuals at Hewlett-Packard; General Electric; Bank of Boston; Blue Cross Blue Shield; Kraft/General Foods; The Ford Foundation; The White House; the Greenville, South Carolina, Housing Authority; Harvard Pilgrim Health Care; and Xerox Corporation.

There are also many groups that have helped support my work in any number of ways. They include the Council on Economic Priorities, the Council on Foreign Relations, the White Plains Public Library, the Scarsdale Public Library, Chappaqua Library, New York Public Library, the Westchester Holocaust Commission, the NAACP, *Jack & Jill,* the *Links,* the Boule, and the Princeton Center for Leadership Training. In particular, I want to thank those individuals who assisted me in my research on the Texaco Corporation.

I am also grateful for the expertise of Jim Childs, Laurie Berger-Morris, Jesica Church, Laurie Frank, Howard Grossman, Monika Jain, Tammy Palazzo,

Acknowledgments

Laurie Sayde-Mehrtens, Cathy Saypol, Perri Dorset, and my editor, Ruth Mills, who believed in this project from the very first time we started investigating the solutions to bias in the workplace.

For her years of friendship, for her business acumen and her willingness to teach me how to develop a unique language for my ideas, I thank my friend and mentor, Judy Marcus.

Through twelve books and innumerable consulting projects, my parents Richard and Betty and my brother Richard have given me the kind of guidance and assistance that is priceless, and I am deeply indebted to them.

And finally, I thank my brilliant wife, Pamela Thomas-Graham, who continues to insist that on the other side of every challenge and every task, there lies a stronger person who can make a difference. It is her optimism, her great intellectual honesty, and her confidence that places me where I need to be.

ABOUT THE AUTHOR

Lawrence Otis Graham is a nationally known author and advisor to companies, nonprofits, government agencies, and other organizations on progressive strategies for managing a changing workplace. He is the author of eleven other books including *Member of the Club* and *The Best Companies for Minorities*.

A graduate of Princeton University and Harvard Law School, Graham is on the faculty of Fordham University where he teaches the course "Minorities and Women in Corporate America." His research has appeared in publications such as *The Wall Street Journal* and *The New York Times*. He has been profiled in *USA Today, Los Angeles Times*, and *Time Magazine*, and he has written numerous articles for such publications as *The New York Times, Business and Society Review, New York Magazine*, and *Executive Citizen*.

In addition to being a member of the Council on Foreign Relations, Graham sits on the boards of the

Council on Economic Priorities and the Princeton Center for Leadership Training. He is a frequent TV commentator on workplace issues and is well-known for his undercover exposes including exposing bias among the corporate elite at a country club in Greenwich, Connecticut.

He is president of Progressive Management Associates, Inc. in White Plains, New York, a consulting firm that has presented workshops, lecture programs, and consulting services to corporate clients and other organizations in the United States and abroad.

Your organization can learn more about Proversity and other workplace programs by contacting Lawrence Otis Graham at:

Progressive Management Associates, Inc.
P.O. Box 316
White Plains, New York 10605
800-776-3201 or 914-949-5400